BASIC READING SERIES

WORKBOOK

LEVEL F

The Purple Turtle

by Donald Rasmussen and Lynn Goldberg

BASIC READING
BERKELEY·CALIFORNIA

To Parents and Teachers

Donald Rasmussen and Lynn Goldberg developed the BASIC READING SERIES (BRS) in the early 1960s at the Miquon School, a small parent-teacher cooperative near Philadelphia. At that time, most children were taught to read using the "sight" or "look-say" method epitomized by the "Dick and Jane" readers, and many were left behind. Don and Lynn knew there must be a better way, so they spent five years developing their own reading program based on the work of the renowned linguist Leonard Bloomfield. They called their method *"inductive whole-word phonics, with a strong linguistics research base."*

After tryouts in inner-city and suburban schools around the country and almost a dozen revisions, the BASIC READING SERIES was published by Science Research Associates (SRA) and enjoyed great success. Over the years, other reading methods have come and then gone out of favor. Now, decades later, phonics is recognized as the scientific approach to reading instruction, and the BASIC READING SERIES is once again available.

BRS is divided into six levels — Levels A to F — with a reader and a workbook for each level. In Level F, children are introduced to r-influenced vowels, such as in *car*, *nor*, and *her*; the "soft" sounds of *c* in *cent*, *g* in *large*, and *s* in *sure*; "silent" letters; infrequent vowel sound-spelling patterns, such as *ou* in *touch*, *ea* in *dead*, and *u* in *pull*; and patterns in which two or more consonants represent a single sound with one or more of the consonants appearing to be silent, such as the *k* in *knee*, the *b* in *dumb*, and the *w* in *wrap*. In addition, the reading selections introduce a number of isolated words spelled in irregular ways, such as *been*, *heart*, *people*, and *women*.

The BRS Workbooks

The workbooks for BRS contain material with which children can practice their decoding skills independently of teacher direction. The decoding experiences thus provided increase the children's opportunities to discover sound-spelling relationships and to develop automatic word recognition. The workbooks are also an aid to vocabulary, word-meaning, and concept development, as they lead children to associate words with appropriate visual images and challenge children to deal with the meanings of words, phrases, and sentences. Finally, the workbooks are a useful tool with which to evaluate the children's decoding progress.

The workbook for Level F has four sections of exercises, which correspond (in their sound-spelling patterns only) to the four sections of the Level F reader, *The Purple Turtle*. The exercises are not tied to the story content of the reader, however. Each section is identified by numbered tabs in the margins of its pages and begins with word charts that present the new words for that section of Level F. Each section progresses from simple exercises based on single words and phrases to more complex exercises involving sentences and short stories.

The workbook is easy to use. Children answer each item in one of four ways: by underlining a word or phrase; by circling a word or phrase; by writing a numeral in a box; or by placing an X in a circle or on an object in the pictures. Since no handwriting skill is needed, the children's reading progress is kept independent of their handwriting progress. The reading lesson can proceed regardless of the children's handwriting abilities.

Some suggestions for the most effective use of the Level F workbook:

1. Do not ask the children to do the work in a given section of the workbook until they have become acquainted with the sound-spelling patterns used in that section. You may want to begin each section of the workbook by reading the word charts for that section with the children. Have the children read up and down the columns, and discuss any unfamiliar words with them before proceeding to the exercises.

2. Throughout the first section of Level F, take care to see that each child understands the directions and is following them correctly before encouraging them to proceed on their own.

3. If a child does not recognize a pictured object, simply tell them what it is.

4. Whenever possible, correct the children's work with them, reading the words, phrases, and sentences aloud and discussing the pictures. The more the children *hear* the words while looking at them, the greater will be their chance to develop automatic word recognition.

5. Try to assess the reasons for the children's errors and deal with them appropriately. Sometimes, as on the riddle pages, an error may be caused by faulty reasoning rather than by faulty decoding. At this stage, accurate decoding is a more important goal than perfect reasoning, and a child who decodes correctly but reasons poorly should still be praised for their reading.

6. Note that there are exercises which are purposely written without clear-cut yes or no answers. These pages should be discussed but not corrected. Either yes or no can be an acceptable answer in many cases. Make it a general rule *for all formats* not to put undue stress on getting the right answer. Instead, put the stress on accurate decoding and the enjoyment of using reading skills in a problem-solving situation.

Copyright © 2024, 2000, 1985, 1976, 1970, 1965, 1964 by the Estates of Donald E. Rasmussen and Lenina Goldberg. All rights reserved. Except as permitted under the United States Copyright Act, no part of this publication may be reproduced or distributed in any form or by any means, or stored in a database or retrieval system, without prior written permission from the publisher.

Email all inquiries to:
Peter Rasmussen, Editor
info@BasicReading.com

Website: BasicReading.com
ISBN 978-1-937547-06-6

1

fair	care	bear	arrow	their
hair	dare	pear	narrow	
pair	fare	tear	sparrow	
chair	hare	wear	■	
stair	share		January	
air	square		February	
■			library	
dairy			■	
fairy			parent	
			■	
			aquarium	

for	door	four	war	more	roar
nor	floor	pour	■	sore	■
or		■	warm	tore	board
■		court	■	wore	
fork			warn	shore	
■			■	store	
fort			dwarf	before	
sort			■		
short			quart		
sport			quarter		
■			quarrel		
born					
corn					
horn					
torn					
■					
morning					

fern	sir	word	fur	afterward
■	■	■	■	forward
clerk	bird	work	burn	upward
■	■	■	turn	orchard
perfect	dirt	worm	return	
■	■	■	■	
perhaps	girl	world	curl	
■	■	■	■	
person	first	worse	hurt	
■	■	■	■	
serve	shirt	worth	purple	
■	■		■	
servant	third		church	
■	■		■	
deserve	thirty		Thursday	
■	■		■	
dessert	thirteen		curve	
■				
verse				

1

dear	deer	sour
fear	cheer	flour
hear	steer	scour
near		our
tear		
year		
clear		
appear		
ear		
■		
beard		

bar	card	barber
car	hard	■
far	yard	garden
jar	■	■
star	lark	pardon
■	mark	■
start	park	March
smart	■	■
chart	farm	market
■	harm	■
harp	■	marble
sharp	barn	■
■	■	farther
scarf	part	■
	apart	alarm

⊗ The farmer is gathering hay with his pitchfork.

○ The farmer is quarreling with the men in the fort.

○ The girl is marking the spot in the garden where the marbles landed.

○ The girl is ordering meat from the merchant at the farmers' market.

○ Mother is saying the girls do not deserve any part of the birthday cake.

○ Mother is presenting Jane with a cake at her birthday party.

○ Arthur is thirsty and is pouring himself a glass of cold milk.

○ Arthur's wife is having a party for him now that he is thirty years old.

○ The boys enjoy playing with their bows and arrows in the park.

○ The boys are taking part in a play and acting on a platform.

○ Father is bringing a board to our home to fix the porch.

○ Father is bringing his shears to cut the flowers on the border of the garden.

1

Their teacher is

- ⊗ marking their report cards.
- ○ marching forward to the clerk.
- ○ curling up in a chair before supper.

Jack likes to see

- ○ sports shows every evening.
- ○ the starch in the curtains.
- ○ the stars when it turns dark.

Pete is sitting in the

- ○ car, waiting for his parents to come.
- ○ barber chair, waiting for a haircut.
- ○ park, waiting for the rain to start.

The hardworking farm girl is

- ○ feeding corn to the pigs in the barnyard.
- ○ planting corn in the garden.
- ○ putting corn into the corncrib.

Martha's car is

- ○ parked near the corner of the yard.
- ○ parked in the shade of the barn.
- ○ parked in the driveway.

When Carmen came to class one Thursday morning, her teacher told her she was late. The teacher said, "There must be some reason why you're so ——."

○ dairy   ⊗ tardy   ○ soapy

They traveled over the dry, hot desert on their horses. The scorching sun made them very ——.

○ thirsty   ○ thirty   ○ third

"May I wear the skirt you got me last year?" asked Margo. . . . "Yes," said Mother, "but I think I will have to lengthen it. When you tried it on last time, you said it was too ——."

○ sharp   ○ shirt   ○ short

Harper was thirteen. He was going shopping at the dairy store for his family. "We need eggs and sour cream," they said. "And get a dessert for Thursday. Here is a quarter for your bus ——."

○ far   ○ first   ○ fare

"Let's pretend we're doctors and nurses today," said one of the children. "We can pretend that we work in a hospital and can treat any boys and girls who are ——."

○ hard   ○ hurt   ○ cheerful

1 Girls can sit on chairs,

but can they sit on stairs?

◯ Yes   ◯ No

A pear can be hard,

but can it be smart?

◯ Yes   ◯ No

A barber can use a pair of shears,

but can he use a pair of tears?

◯ Yes   ◯ No

A man can be short,

but can he be a sport?

◯ Yes   ◯ No

Dad can drive in a car,

but can he drive very far?

◯ Yes   ◯ No

A scarf is something to wear,

but is it something to tear?

◯ Yes   ◯ No

A man can row his boat to shore,

but can he row it to a store?

◯ Yes   ◯ No

A person can be a nurse,

but can a person be a verse?

◯ Yes   ◯ No

"I'm bored," Kim said to her big brother on a Thursday morning. "I would love to go camping and enjoy the wildlife. We could see hares and bears, larks and sparrows and deer."

Then Kim stopped and said, "The only problem is that it's January, the coldest month of the year."

"No problem," Jimmy replied. "Let's ask our parents to take us camping when it's warmer outside. Perhaps we should delay our trip until summer, when it's warm."

"That's a fine plan," said Kim. "I can't wait to go!"

Draw an X to show when Kim and Jimmy should go camping.

Craig's big brother, Don, was home from the army. He had many stories to tell.

"Each morning," said Don, "I would blow a horn to awaken everyone."

"Then," he added, "we dressed, went outdoors, and marched around."

"Afterward we ate our food and prepared to do some drilling."

Craig and his brother agreed that being in the army is hard work, but it can be fun if each man takes part in the chores.

Put an X on the thing Don used to awaken everyone each morning.

1

○ Jane is feeding the four fish in her aquarium.

○ Jane is setting the clock so that the alarm will ring at four.

○ Jill is brushing her hair to make it curl.

○ Jill is jumping on the chair, but she isn't harming it.

○ Clark is tearing his shirt as he turns the corner.

○ Clark is rubbing his arm after he fell off the chair.

○ Each girl has a curl in the middle of her forehead.

○ Each girl tore out her hair when the team was beaten.

○ Paul is pouring a quart of oil into the car.

○ Jack is parking his car in the yard.

○ The girls are cheerful in spite of the bad scare.

○ Barbara is cheering for the girls on her team.

If you are afraid of something, you can say you have a ☐1☐.

1. fear   2. cheer

If you want two of something, you may order a ☐.

1. part   2. pair

To keep your neck warm on cold days, you sometimes wear a ☐.

1. scarf   2. shirt

In the evening farmers put their animals into a ☐.

1. barn   2. born

My dog Superstar barks whenever she hears the ☐.

1. doorstep   2. doorbell

One of the birds that stays in the North in the winter is the ☐.

1. sparrow   2. stairs

When a dog hears something odd or hears loud sounds, it begins to ☐.

1. park   2. bark

Every year on my birthday we bake a cake and we have a ☐.

1. party   2. pear

A farmer may use a scarecrow in the orchard to scare away the ☐.

1. blackboards   2. blackbirds

When we see the sun in the morning, we are very ☐.

1. cheerful   2. queer

1

On a clear day in February, Lora and her pals were playing in the park. One of Lora's pals said, "Let's pretend to hunt bears. We can hunt them with our bows and ———."

○ airplanes   ○ arrows   ○ aquariums

Carla's teacher returned the spelling papers to the class. "Your paper was perfect," she told Carla. "You'll be able to show your parents a fine report ———."

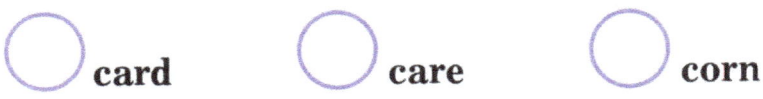

○ card   ○ care   ○ corn

"Harry, I think perhaps it's time you had a haircut," said Father. Harry was happy to go. He liked sitting in the barber chair and hearing the sound of the snapping ———.

○ servants   ○ shears   ○ stars

Doris and Cathy March saw the moon and the stars on a clear evening. Afterward, when they were in bed, Doris said to Cathy, "When we awaken in the morning, the moon and stars will have ———."

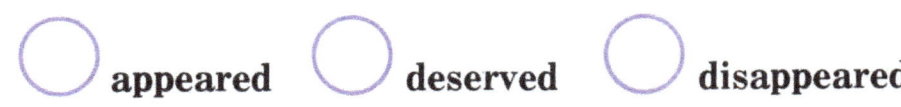

○ appeared   ○ deserved   ○ disappeared

Mark Lopez neatly and carefully piled his shirts on his bed. He put one on and said, "I can barely button this collar." Mother said, "Perhaps the cleaners have used too much ———."

○ scorch   ○ squares   ○ starch

1

Butter can be burned,

but can it be churned?

○ Yes ○ No

A curtain can be torn,

but can it be worn?

○ Yes ○ No

A church can have a floor,

but can it have a door?

○ Yes ○ No

A girl can wear a shirt,

but can she wear a skirt?

○ Yes ○ No

A bottle can hold a quart,

but can it hold a court?

○ Yes ○ No

If you're hurt, you can get worse;

but can you get a nurse?

○ Yes ○ No

A car can be parked in a yard;

can it be parked in a card?

○ Yes ○ No

Flour can be poured,

but can it be stored?

○ Yes ○ No

1

"This Thursday will be your birthday," Mother said to Marsha.

"Will I be able to have a party?" asked Marsha.

Mother said yes, and Marsha cheerfully started to make her plans.

On Thursday when the children arrived, some began to play a game. Bob pinned a tail on the pony's nose. Others sat down to sing.

Mother had prepared strawberry shortcake, and she served it to the children.

Afterward Marsha said she had enjoyed her party very much.

Put an X on the spot where Bob pinned the pony's tail.

One day Marty and Barbie made several birthday cards.

"We can sit at Father's workbench and make the cards in many sizes, some wide and some narrow," said Marty.

When Mother saw them, she agreed that the artwork on the cards was perfect, and that the cards were worth having.

"I know that you both worked very hard to make these fine cards," said Mother.

Marty had made a pair of cards to match. Each one had a wide border of flowers. Barbie had made a square one with a border of purple hearts.

Put an X on the card that Barbie made.

In October under the big oak tree we find many ☐.

1. acorns   2. arrows

The three animals that Goldilocks met in the story were ☐.

1. bears   2. barns

We ran to turn in a fire alarm when we found that the store was ☐.

1. barking   2. burning

The stems of the roses in my parents' garden have many ☐.

1. thorns   2. horns

Before we go to sleep, we like to hear Father tell a ☐.

1. stork   2. story

Stairs that are not wide are ☐.

1. near   2. narrow

The man who helps us with our bags when we get off a train is a ☐.

1. porter   2. porch

When I was hurt and in a hospital, the person who cared for me was a ☐.

1. nurse   2. north

You can harm a tree if you cut off its ☐.

1. bark   2. beard

Storks, larks, and sparrows are birds that fly in the ☐.

1. air   2. art

1

One day when Ken was outdoors playing in the garden, he found a turtle.

"Perhaps you're thirsty," said Ken. "I'll get you something to drink and some food."

Afterward the turtle appeared behind Ken wherever Ken went.

"You're really not the sort of pet I wanted," said Ken, "but I will keep you in a jar on the floor of our porch."

1. What do you think the turtle will do?
   - ○ He will turn into a scarecrow.
   - ○ He will live happily in his jar.

2. What do you think the turtle said?
   - ○ "I can be a harmful pal."
   - ○ "Thank you, sir. I like to be near you."

3. What do you think Ken said?
   - ○ "I wish you had curly hair."
   - ○ "I didn't want you before, but now I like you."

One afternoon when Donna was playing outdoors, she found a purse on the street.

"Perhaps if I open the purse carefully," said Donna, "I will find out who owns it."

She found that the owner's name was Ms. Star, and she started out to return the purse. Standing on the doorstep, Donna rang the doorbell. A lady came to the door and said, "What can I do for you, Miss?"

1. What do you think Donna said?
   - ○ "I've come to return your purse."
   - ○ "I've come to report a harmful person."

2. What do you think Ms. Star said?
   - ○ "Ladies don't carry purses."
   - ○ "I didn't know my purse had disappeared."

3. What do you think Ms. Star did?
   - ○ She invited Donna inside to share some shortcake.
   - ○ She scared Donna by wearing a purple skirt.

Draw a line under anything that can be torn.

a shirt	a chart
a card	a stork
a star	a scarf

Draw a line under anything that can be found on a farm.

a barn	a pear orchard
fairies	armies
ears of corn	a farmer

Draw a line under anything that can be found in a store.

a war	a bear
a clerk	a girl
a merchant	a chair

Draw a line under anything that can be warmed.

corn	pork
a tart	butter
an arrow	a hair

Draw a line under anything that can be poured into a jar.

flour	warm milk
cars	sour cream
curtains	kernels of corn

Draw a line under anything that can get dirty.

a skirt	a bird
a year	a cheer
a sore	a store

Draw a line under anything that can be found in a kindergarten classroom.

a blackboard	a rainstorm
a park	a door
girls	chairs

Draw a line under anything that can get thirsty.

a person	a chair
a bird	a hare
the stairs	a deer

1

If your father's working

If your father's working in a store, what could he be?

- ⊗ a clerk
- ○ an airman
- ○ a farmer

If your father's working in a food market, what could he sell?

- ○ corn on the cob
- ○ purple turtles
- ○ girls' skirts

If your father's working in a barbershop, what could he do?

- ○ repair curls
- ○ cut hair
- ○ march in a parade

If your father isn't working

If your father isn't working, what could he do in the park?

- ○ return Mother's purse
- ○ rest on a park bench
- ○ order a shortcake

If your father isn't working, what could he do in a church?

- ○ shave a scarecrow
- ○ start a snowstorm
- ○ play an organ

If your father isn't working, what could he do in his armchair?

- ○ read a story
- ○ scour the floor
- ○ fix his car

What's the story about?

Every three weeks I go to the barbershop for a haircut. I sit on a chair, and the barber carefully cuts my hair with his shears.

One day I said jokingly to my barber, Mr. Court, "You may also shave my beard."

"You have many years to go, Don, before you will need a shave," Mr. Court said. "But we will pretend that you are grown, and I will put soap on your beard to prepare for the shave."

"What a funny feeling," I said as I pretended.

"There," said Mr. Court. "I have finished your shave and haircut. I'll see you in three weeks."

○ The Barber Cuts a Beard

⊗ A Funny Shave at the Barbershop

○ A Harmful Cut at the Barbershop

One morning Martin Miller and his parents went to the airport. They were taking a trip to a northern state to visit Martin's grandmother and grandfather. Before boarding the airplane, Martin counted thirteen other planes parked at the airport.

"We have a perfect day for flying," the pilot said to Martin when they had boarded. "Perhaps you'd like to sit up with me later."

Soon Martin could feel the plane take off. Afterward he sat beside the pilot. The sky was clear, and the world below seemed tiny. In a while they reached the airport in the northern state, and the pilot landed the plane. The trip was short, but it was fun.

○ A Disappearing Airplane Trick

○ An Interesting Airplane Trip

○ An Alarming Airplane Trip

1

A barber may cut hair,

    but can he cut the air?

◯ Yes   ◯ No

A man can own an arrow;

    can he also own a narrow?

◯ Yes   ◯ No

A man can take a share;

    can he also take a dare?

◯ Yes   ◯ No

You can share a pear,

    but can you share a square?

◯ Yes   ◯ No

Mom can stitch a shirt;

    can she also stitch some dirt?

◯ Yes   ◯ No

A person can own a store,

    but can a person own a shore?

◯ Yes   ◯ No

A cow could eat some corn,

    but could it eat a horn?

◯ Yes   ◯ No

A lemon may taste sour,

    but can it taste like flour?

◯ Yes   ◯ No

The beds in the hospital are ☐ and are cared for by the ☐.

1. nurses   2. narrow

We ☐ to have dinner at our home when father ☐ the soup.

1. serves   2. start

For her ☐, Ann asked for the biggest ☐ in the store.

1. birthday   2. blackboard

When you ☐ hard, you may get very ☐.

1. warm   2. work

Father does not like to wear a ☐ that has any ☐ in it.

1. starch   2. shirt

Every ☐ we go to the library and select ☐ interesting stories for our class.

1. Thursday   2. thirteen

Each ☐ had to take a turn standing on a ☐ to tell a story.

1. person   2. platform

Mrs. March works in the ☐ and is the happiest ☐ I know.

1. merchant   2. market

I drive slowly around a ☐ and I'm ☐ as I turn.

1. corner   2. careful

It is fun for a ☐ to compete in ☐ and win.

1. sports   2. girl

19

1

This is a story about an elf. He appeared out of thin air in Jane's bedroom when it was dark. He wore a pointed cap and pointed slippers. His ears were shaped like a bear's, and he had a beard.

"I'm a pal, and I've come to serve you," said the elf. "Make three wishes, and in the morning they will be granted."

"You make your wishes," said the elf, "and mark my word—in the morning they will be granted." Then he disappeared.

1. What do you think Jane did before she fell asleep?
○ She marked three worms.
○ She made three wishes.

2. What do you think Jane wished for?
○ She wished for a teddy bear, a turtle, and a bird.
○ She wished for a sour apple and a torn shirt.

3. What happened the next morning?
○ Jane met the elf and quarreled with him.
○ Jane found a teddy bear, a turtle, and a bird.

At her window one morning, Nora could see the bird feeder her parents had put on a branch of their oak tree. It appeared that a blackbird and a sparrow were quarreling there. Nora could hear their sharp sounds clearly.

"There's plenty of seed for both of you, Mr. Blackbird and Mr. Sparrow. You must share the food, and you must not quarrel anymore," Nora warned.

1. What do you think the sparrow said?
○ "I got here first. I deserve the food."
○ "Nora is warning you that she'll harm you."

2. After Nora's warning, what do you think the blackbird said?
○ "I don't care for birdseed."
○ "O.K., Mr. Sparrow, let's share the birdseed."

3. What do you think Nora did afterward?
○ She put more birdseed in the bird feeder.
○ She allowed the birds to settle their quarrel.

Draw a line under anything that can be worn.

a garden   a scarf

a deer   a curl

a shirt   a hair

Draw a line under anything that is hard.

dirt   a deer

sour milk   a marble

flour   a quarter

Draw a line under anything that can be eaten.

hair   corn

a pear   a fork

a park   a scarecrow

Draw a line under anything that you can get at a market.

a bird feeder   corn

a parent   flour

a chair   a shore

Draw a line under anything that has hair.

a chair   a sparrow

a bear   a beard

a fairy   a barber

Draw a line under anything that would make people laugh.

a clown   a baby

a board   a curtain

a joke   a snore

Draw a line under anything that can be found on a playground.

beds   swings

children   bacon

grass   teachers

Draw a line under anything that can fly.

an airplane   a stork

a horsefly   a purse

a turtle   a worm

What's the story about?

1

When Jill was thirteen years old, her parents told her she could select her own skirts and dresses. She went to the store alone for the first time. She asked the clerk whether he had the kind of skirt she wanted.

"I'll be happy to help you," the salesclerk said politely. Jill tried on many skirts. Some were too short, and others were too narrow at the waist. Finally she found the perfect skirt, and a shirt too. She also selected a purse and a scarf while she was there. She returned home cheerfully. Her parents said she had done very well alone, and they were proud of her.

○ Jill Selects a Scarf

○ A Salesclerk Greets Jill

○ Jill's First Shopping Trip

Martha smelled smoke one morning and awakened both her parents. They ran outdoors and found that their barn was burning and that the corn they had stored in it was burning.

"Hurry and turn in a fire alarm!" cried Martha's dad.

This was the worst fire Martha had ever seen. The flames leaped into the air. Before help came, Martha and her parents tried to put out the fire in the burning barn. But the flames had harmed most of their corn. Some of it, however, was unharmed.

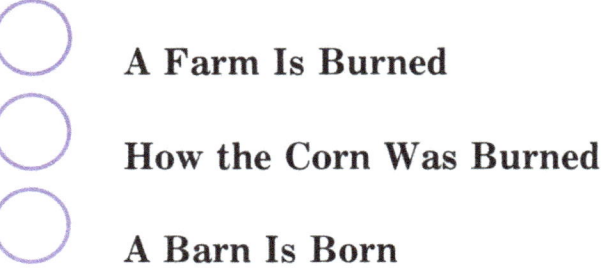

○ A Farm Is Burned

○ How the Corn Was Burned

○ A Barn Is Born

I stand next to a chair.

I cut men's hair.

I use shears in my work.

Am I — (a barber) / a blackbird / a board ?

I own a big barn.

I grow many crops and sell them at the market.

I have dairy cows.

Am I — a fern / a farmer / a floor ?

It makes a loud sound.

Most cars have one.

Ships need it in the dark and in storms.

Is it — a hair / a hare / a horn ?

A Trip down the River

1

One day in March, Karl and Burt, pretending to be sailors, loaded food onto a raft and started on a trip down the river. They wanted to sail to faraway ports to see some more of the world. A short time later they were in a thick fog.

"I'm afraid we'll never find the shore," said Karl.

"Have no fear," said Burt. "The fog will soon disappear. Then we'll find the shore. Till the fog lifts we must be careful."

As the boys spoke, the fog seemed to lift somewhat. They could make out the forms of trees on the shore. Then the sun appeared.

"Let's see the chart," said Karl, "so we can find out where we are."

Karl carefully unrolled the chart. "Here is where we are," he said, pointing to a clearly marked spot.

"If we work hard," said Burt, "we can be home soon."

They rowed their raft in the dark until morning, when they finally arrived home. They returned home unharmed but were very thirsty and cold. Their parents were overjoyed to see them but made them say that they would never take the raft out alone anymore.

	Yes	No
1. The boys went on their trip so that they could see more of the world.	⊗	○
2. The fog appeared before they started, so they couldn't go.	○	○
3. Burt said that the fog would never disappear and things would get worse.	○	○
4. An old man gave the boys a chart to help them find their way home.	○	○
5. When the boys turned back, the fog reappeared, and the boys could not get home.	○	○
6. The boys had to row hard to get home.	○	○

Everyone has two of them.

They help you hear.

They can disappear under a girl's scarf.

Are they
- ears
- eggs
- arms

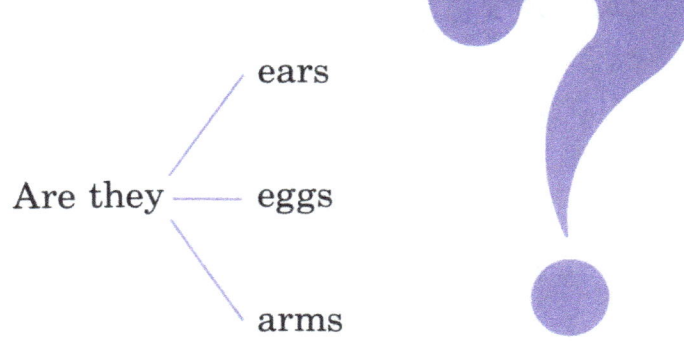

Farmers' wives can pack jams and jellies in it.

You have to turn its top to open it.

It can be short and can fit on a corner shelf.

Is it
- a war
- a jar
- a fur

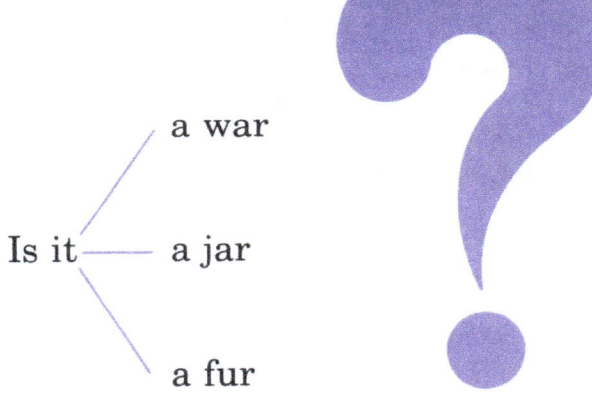

It is glass and is shaped like a box.

Fish swim in it, and you cannot let it get dirty.

You can keep snails and shells in it.

Is it
- an alarm
- an aquarium
- an acorn

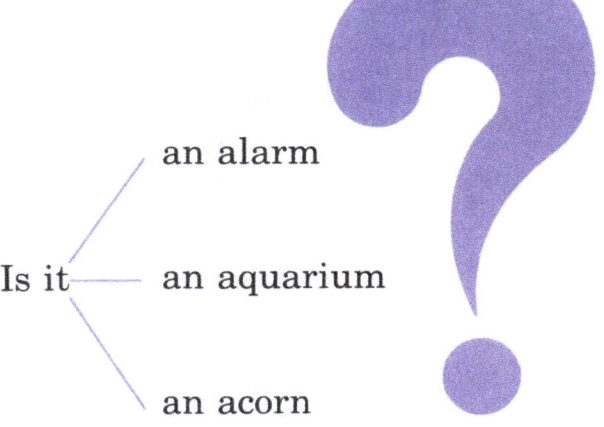

2

ball call tall small all ■ almost ■ also ■ always ■ salt	cost lost ■ cross across ■ song long belong strong ■ soft ■ coffee ■ chocolate ■ gone	broad	pause cause because

breeze freeze sneeze squeeze ■ cheese ■ geese	chief thief ■ field ■ believe	leave weave ■ please disease ■ breathe ■ increase	sardine ■ gasoline ■ automobile	seize ■ either

blue glue true ■ cruel ■ value ■ Tuesday	new blew chew drew flew grew screw threw ■ few	suit fruit	move remove ■ lose	goose loose ■ choose	shoe canoe

give live forgive ■ native ■ promise ■ opposite	busy ■ business	build ■ built

son won ■ month ■ money ■ Monday ■ among ■ color ■ cover ■ company ■ nothing	love dove glove above	double trouble ■ touch ■ young ■ cousin ■ country ■ southern	blood flood

2

dead	else	guess	again	friend	bury
head	■	■	■		
read	sense	guest	against		
bread					
■					
ready					
■					
feather					
weather					
■					
instead					
■					
meant					
■					
heavy					
■					
sweater					
■					
breakfast					

book	bush	wolf
cook	push	■
took	■	woman
shook	cushion	
■	■	
cooky	full	
■	pull	
good	■	
wood	bulletin	
stood	■	
■	pudding	
foot	■	
■	butcher	
wool	■	
	during	

○ Jill's new coat has a warm fur-lined hood.

○ Jill is hanging up her new coat in the hallway.

○ Wanda and Donna are tossing the cushions, and many feathers are flying.

○ Wanda and Donna are throwing the soft cloth into the freezer.

○ Mom is hooking up the horn to the gasoline tank.

○ Mom is honking the horn, and a girl is coming over to put gasoline in the car.

○ Walter and his grandpa have lost the tall table in the room.

○ Walter and his grandpa are moving the heavy table across the room.

○ Howard is touching the walrus and finding it friendly.

○ Howard is taking the walrus outside to touch the leaves.

○ Richard is washing the mouse in a bathtub of cheese.

○ Richard is watching the mouse nibble on the cheese.

Tomas is putting his books in the
- ○ butcher shop where they belong.
- ○ woolen bookstore that he built.
- ○ wooden bookcase that he built.

Jo is very busy
- ○ cooking spinach for breakfast.
- ○ baking her chocolate cookies.
- ○ buying chocolate-frosted cookies.

Cooky and her grandma agree that
- ○ the mouse they seize will be a friend.
- ○ the birdhouse they built is strong.
- ○ the washbowl they built is strong.

The thief is running from the store
- ○ with the cheese under his arm.
- ○ to the front seat of an automobile.
- ○ as the storekeeper shouts for help.

Jed has put the money on the counter and
- ○ is asking for the cookies.
- ○ is putting on his new sweater.
- ○ is ordering breakfast.

Do you believe that Santa's reindeer can really fly in the air? If they could be seen, children all over the world would be ———.

○ pleased   ○ squeezed   ○ strong

2

Father said to his son Don, "You have grown so much that now you can work and make money by selling ———."

○ breakfast   ○ nothing   ○ newspapers

Jack Wong had grown tall, and his shoulders were broad. One day Mother said, "Jack, I guess it would be a good idea to buy you a new wool ———."

○ sardine   ○ salt   ○ suit

"I always enjoy reading the many books my parents give me. When I have read them all, I can buy more at the ———."

○ bookstore   ○ broadcast   ○ bulletin

My twin sister and I are alike. When people watch us at play, they think they are seeing ———.

○ diamonds   ○ double   ○ diseases

2

A mouse loves to eat cheese.

Does it love to freeze?

◯ **Yes**   ◯ **No**

A fish can be hooked.

Can it also be cooked?

◯ **Yes**   ◯ **No**

People can wear suits.

Can they also wear fruits?

◯ **Yes**   ◯ **No**

A book can be read.

Can it also be read?

◯ **Yes**   ◯ **No**

Small children can be raised.

Can they also be praised?

◯ **Yes**   ◯ **No**

Mom can paddle her canoe.

Can she paddle her soft shoe?

◯ **Yes**   ◯ **No**

A song can be long.

Can it also be strong?

◯ **Yes**   ◯ **No**

Bees can give us honey.

Can they also give us money?

◯ **Yes**   ◯ **No**

Mother and Jane went to see the shoemaker. He was busy repairing a pair of shoes.

There were all kinds of shoes in the store. Some were big, for grown people, and some were small, for young people.

In the front of the store were all kinds of newspapers for people to read while waiting for their shoes to be fixed.

It was fun to watch the shoemaker hammer new soles on shoes. But Mother and Jane stayed only a minute, for they had more shopping that had to be done.

Put an X on the things people read while they wait for their shoes to be fixed.

Dick Smith went to the country to visit his cousin Dan. Dan lived on a farm and this was the first time Dick had seen many things found on a farm. He saw fields of corn and a hundred pigs to eat it. He saw the dairy barn where the cows were fed and milked. And he saw a flock of sheep with their woolly coats. But what interested Dick the most was the people he met on the farm. They seemed as friendly as any people he had ever met.

Put an X on what Dick found most interesting on the farm.

2

If you catch a cold, you may begin to ☐.

1. breeze 2. sneeze

One thing I really like to do is read a ☐.

1. cooky 2. book

We couldn't go on a picnic because of the bad ☐.

1. feather 2. weather

Mom said that after dinner we could have some chocolate ☐.

1. pudding 2. bushes

When it's cold outside, you should wear ☐.

1. gloves 2. doves

Before you go out in the morning, you should eat ☐.

1. breakfast 2. sweaters

The baby can't go with us; she's too ☐.

1. young 2. cousin

The first day of the week is ☐.

1. Monday 2. money

I have to clean the house because we are going to have a ☐.

1. guest 2. guess

In the country you can sometimes see cows grazing in the ☐.

1. chiefs 2. fields

34

○ Little Red Riding Hood is behind the bushes because she sees the big bad wolf.

○ Little Red Riding Hood is taking the bread out of her basket.

○ Robert has tiny sardines for breakfast before he goes fishing.

○ Robert has a fish as small as a sardine on his line.

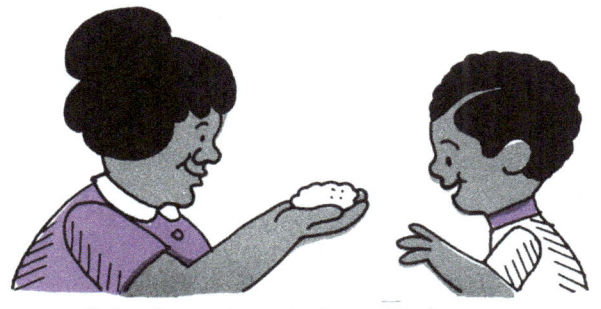

○ Mother is giving Bob a cookie for helping to pick the fruit.

○ Mother is giving Bob a jacket for eating all the fruit.

○ The airman is the tallest man in the field.

○ The field is filled with rows of tall corn.

○ Judy's mother always has an egg for breakfast.

○ Judy's mother always has chocolate cake for breakfast.

○ James is having cookies and pudding for his breakfast.

○ James prefers fruit and bread for his breakfast.

2

The radio was on, and soft music was playing. Suddenly Father said to us, "I must hear the weather ———."

 report    remove    return

"I have a good idea for a pleasant day," father said. "Let's invite your cousins to go on a picnic in the ———."

 money    brook    meadow

"May I help get breakfast ready?" asked Bart. "Yes, thanks," said mother. "Would you please toast the rye ———?"

 breath    bread    brook

Father told me many stories about Grandma when she was a young woman. "Most of all she enjoyed weaving," said Father. "In that way she made her own ———."

 chocolate    country    cloth

"I have a surprise for you," our teacher said one morning. "On Tuesday our class will be guests at the puppet show being held at the ———."

mousetrap    playhouse    broadcast

36

Monkeys can swing and fall.

Can they also yell and call?

◯ Yes   ◯ No

A field can be crossed.

Can a field also be tossed?

◯ Yes   ◯ No

Young women can give presents.

Can they also be pleasant?

◯ Yes   ◯ No

Woodpeckers fly in the sky above.

Can they fly inside a glove?

◯ Yes   ◯ No

A needle can be threaded.

Can a needle also be breaded?

◯ Yes   ◯ No

A small boy can squeeze.

Can a small boy also sneeze?

◯ Yes   ◯ No

We make sweaters out of wool.

Do we make leather out of wool?

◯ Yes   ◯ No

Cats can mew.

Can they also chew?

◯ Yes   ◯ No

2

I don't like to be sick at all, but what I hate most is having a cold.

My mother always makes me stay in bed when I have a cold, so I won't give it to anyone else in the family.

I take all my toys to bed with me. The one I enjoy most is my teddy bear. But I hate to stay in bed, even when I have my toys.

I am always happy a few days later when I feel well again and can leave my bed.

Put an X on the toy the boy enjoys most when he has a cold.

One day Bob and Margo were tossing a ball against the house. Margo said, "Bob, why don't we do something else? Either we could make a scrapbook or we could build a clubhouse."

Bob said a clubhouse was a great idea, so they began to build one. First Margo piled some crates in stacks for walls. Then Bob put boards across the crates.

It was not a very tall building, and the room inside was small. When Bob stood up in the clubhouse his head scraped the top. He was an inch too tall.

He said, "Maybe it would help if I removed my shoes."

Put an X on the child who built the walls.

If you were a mouse, you would like to eat ☐.

1. cheese   2. chiefs

Some caterpillars turn into butterflies, and some become ☐.

1. moths   2. months

When you ask for something, you should use the word ☐.

1. because   2. please

One of the most pleasant things people can do as a group is sing ☐.

1. songs   2. sons

In the morning the grass on a lawn is sometimes covered with drops of ☐.

1. news   2. dew

If you help your dad build a bulletin board, you'll need wood, nails, and ☐.

1. squirrels   2. screws

When you have a checkup by your family doctor, he may ask you to stick out your ☐.

1. touch   2. tongue

We all know that automobiles can't move without ☐.

1. gasoline   2. glue

If you try to use buttons to buy candy at the store, you'll soon find out that you need ☐.

1. money   2. minutes

The king needed new shoes, so he went to the ☐.

1. shoemaker   2. woodcutter

39

2

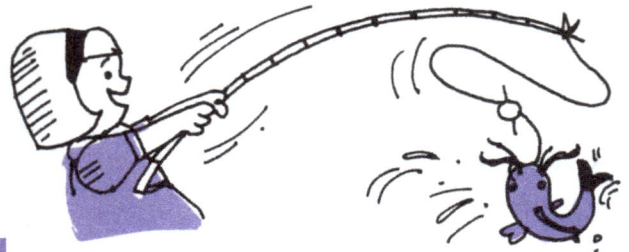

During the summer months, Marion and her father spent many pleasant days fishing. They started out before breakfast, because the trip to the brook took a long time. When they reached the brook, dad showed Marion how to put a hook on her line. She threw the line into the brook, and before long Marion felt something pulling on her line.

"Hurrah! I must have hooked a fish!" Marion shouted.

Marion was proud of the small catfish she pulled in.

1. What did Marion's father do?
   ○ He showed Marion how to hook an old shoe.
   ○ He took Marion to a brook to go fishing.

2. What do you think Marion said?
   ○ "Let's take this fish home and cook it for dinner."
   ○ "That goose has lovely feathers."

3. What do you think Marion and her father did?
   ○ They took the fish home.
   ○ They agreed never to go fishing again.

Carmela liked going to Grandma's house, because Grandma always let her bake cookies.

"Today, Grandma, it would be fun to surprise Grandpa with chocolate brownies," said Carmela.

"What a great idea," Grandma agreed. "We'll make several dozen brownies, and you may take some home with you for your mother and father."

Carmela helped her grandma prepare the mix and put the batch of brownies in the oven.

1. What did Carmela do when the brownies were ready?
   ○ She threw them away.
   ○ She removed them from the oven.

2. What do you think Carmela said?
   ○ "Let's visit Washington."
   ○ "May I come again and bake some more brownies?"

3. What do you think Grandma said?
   ○ "You may come next Tuesday."
   ○ "Washington has good weather this month."

Draw a line under anything that you can cook.

breakfast	pudding
socks	spinach
a goose	a jacket

Draw a line under anything that you can buy.

praise	a sneeze
a snowman	a pair of shoes
grandma	a sewing kit

Draw a line under anything you can chew.

rye bread	a chocolate bar
cheesecake	leather
a watch	an onion

Draw a line under anything you would use only in cold weather.

woolen gloves	a heavy jacket
a warm hood	chewing gum
a newspaper	a snowsuit

Draw a line under anything your parents would buy for you.

a reindeer	a book
a scrapbook	leather gloves
a football	a brownie

Draw a line under anything you can make out of wood.

a suit	a cup of tea
a bookcase	a playhouse
a wall	a song

Draw a line under anything too heavy to move by yourself.

a catfish	a watermelon
a jar of honey	an automobile
a wall	a dozen shovels

Draw a line under anything that is smaller than you.

a wasp	a gasoline tank
a meadow	a mouse
an onion	a cushion

What's the story about?

Linda read the story of Little Red Riding Hood and the big bad wolf many times. She read that Little Red Riding Hood mistook the wolf for her grandma.

"What a dreadful thing to happen," said Linda. "When I go wandering in the meadow, I will never trust any wolf, for it appears to me that they're cruel to young children. Of course, there are many pleasant and friendly animals living in the woods. They are ready to be our friends."

Then she added, "I'd choose a woodpecker to be my friend."

○ Little Red Riding Hood

○ The Wolf Meets Linda

○ What Linda Thinks about Wolves

Do you know the story about the walrus who was a native of the North Pole? He had read books about the warm weather in other parts of the world. So one day he waved goodbye to all his walrus friends. He wanted to travel to a southern country.

He wandered for several months and crossed snow-covered lands. The breezes grew warmer and warmer, and his fur coat seemed heavier and heavier. He missed his friends and was truly sorry that he had left the North Pole.

It would be a long trip back, but the trip would be worthwhile, for he would be back among his friends.

○ The Wandering Walrus

○ The Walrus Meets a Friend

○ The Walrus Turns into a Washbowl

Mother will call Charlie when she is ☐ to ☐ the book to him.

1. ready   2. read

If you ☐ a feather pillow, you will find that it makes some people ☐.

1. squeeze   2. sneeze

Father found his newspaper ☐ the books, and he ☐ found his glasses.

1. among   2. also

If you take a deep ☐ outside, you will sometimes enjoy the fresh ☐.

1. breath   2. breeze

Grandma makes hot ☐ for me, but ☐ for Mama and Papa.

1. coffee   2. chocolate

Sometimes when Mother is very ☐, she drops things and ☐ them.

1. busy   2. breaks

Some children may find it hard to ☐ between a ☐ sandwich and a cooky.

1. choose   2. cheese

It would be no ☐ to see a ☐ pick up a walnut.

1. surprise   2. squirrel

Ezra ☐ his mother and ran to the store to ☐ a quart of milk.

1. buy   2. obeyed

You should use your own ☐ ☐ of someone else's.

1. instead   2. ideas

43

2

Draw a line under anything you can lift.

a wolf	an automobile
a cushion	a goose
a feather	a sneeze

Draw a line under anything found in a house.

a thief	a wolf
a kitten	a field of corn
a woman	an automobile

Draw a line under anything that runs.

a wolf	glue
blood	a business
a shoe	an automobile

Draw a line under anything that grows.

a sardine	fruit
a song	trouble
a goose	love

Draw a line under anything that can be found in a classroom.

cookies	trouble
breakfast	a canoe
friends	a pot of glue

Draw a line under anything that moves by itself.

a shoe	a book
a woman	a field
a cross	a butcher

Draw a line under anything that fits in a pocketbook.

a sardine	a pair of gloves
a cup of tea	a stocking cap
a guest	a rosebush

Draw a line under anything that is heavier than you.

your friend	a butcher shop
a dove	a woman
a feather	your feet

What's the story about?

If I could be a fairy, I would grant everybody's wishes. I think Mama would wish for all people to be kind to each other. Papa would choose to have the world free of disease. My sister Jane would want either a new playhouse or a pair of shoes like Mother's. Brother Jack is very young, but I would also grant him a wish. Perhaps he already has all he wants, but I believe I would give him a new soft toy to squeeze. If I could be a fairy, I would still have more wishes to grant, because a fairy never uses up all her wishes.

○ I Wish I Could Be a Fairy

○ What I Would Do if I Were a Fairy

○ The Fairy's Family

Ray wanted to be able to read the newspaper. He had trouble, however, because he was so young and didn't know all the words. He found that the best idea was to ask his mother, if she was not too busy, to read the news with him. He liked to know all about the weather, because it helped him to know whether he should wear a sweater outdoors. He liked to know about baseball teams, because baseball was interesting. But most of all, Ray liked to know what people were doing all over the world. Soon Ray will be able to read a newspaper by himself, for he already reads many words.

○ A Boy Removes the News

○ A Boy Reads a Newspaper

○ A Boy Returns the Newspaper

2

What would you buy?

If you were a shoemaker, what would you buy?

○ a heavy sweater
○ a lot of leather
○ a leather feather

If you were a farmer, what would you build?

○ a blue firehouse
○ a big barn
○ a leaky canoe

If you were a woodcutter, what would you buy?

○ a woodpecker
○ a scrapbook
○ a truck to move wood

What wouldn't you buy?

If you were a cook, what wouldn't you buy?

○ some chocolate glue
○ a push-button oven
○ a new cookbook

If you were a grandma, what wouldn't you buy?

○ a basketball
○ a baseball
○ a weather broadcast

If you were a tailor, what wouldn't you buy?

○ a can of gasoline
○ a sewing kit
○ a spool of thread

I Like to Pretend.

It is fine to be a person, but I guess some people think of being something else. If I could be a glove, I believe I would be a warm woolen glove. When you wore me, your hand would not freeze. If you were playing in the snow, you could throw many snowballs and build many big snowhouses.

If I could be a cushion, I believe I would choose to be a small, soft cushion filled with all kinds of feathers. You could put me against a chair and rest your shoulders on me. You could toss me into the air and catch me when I fell.

If I could be a scrapbook, I would choose to be a great big scrapbook. You could glue many things in me. When you read me, you would find many pleasant things inside me.

If I could be a house, I would choose to be a playhouse for you and your friends. You could build many things for me. I would be no trouble to keep clean because I would be small, and in a few minutes everything could be put where it belonged.

But I believe it is still the most fun to be a person. A person can wear a warm woolen glove. A person can use a small soft cushion. A person can read a great big scrapbook and play in a playhouse. Yes, being a person is the most fun.

		Yes	No
1.	If I chose to be a scrapbook, I would be a very small one, so that only a few things could be glued inside me.	○	○
2.	If I were a woolen glove, your hand would freeze inside me.	○	○
3.	If I were a cushion, you could lean your shoulders against me or toss me into the air.	○	○
4.	If I chose to be a house, I would be a great, tall brick house with many loose windows.	○	○
5.	If I were a playhouse, I would be small and easy to clean.	○	○
6.	I think the most fun is being a monkey.	○	○

2 It has four tires.

It needs gasoline to make it go.

It is built of strong materials.

Is it — a diamond / an automobile / a newspaper

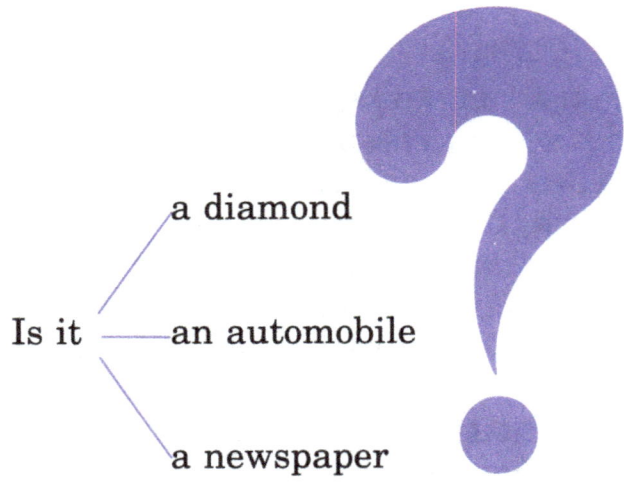

It has dozens and dozens of seeds in it.

Children love to eat it.

It is heavy to pick up before it is cut.

Is it — a watermelon / a walnut / a feather

Some people spread it on bread.

It has a sweet, pleasant taste.

It is found in a hive.

Is it — cheese / honey / butter

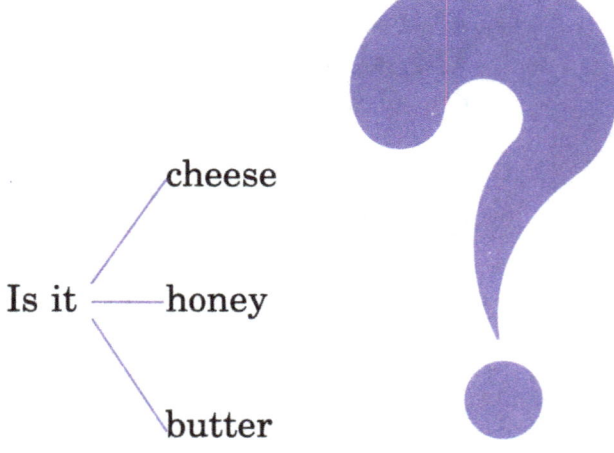

The Young Acting Company

One summer morning Sarah and a few of her friends agreed that it would be fun to find something different to do.

"We could put on a show in my backyard, and our families and friends could come to see us. We could call ourselves the Young Acting Company."

"Because this is your idea," said one of her friends, "we'll make you our chief, and we'll obey your wishes." Her other friends agreed.

"Well," said Sarah, "first I'll call my big brother Jack. He's a great carpenter. I know he'll build us a playhouse if I ask him to. Then we can go to the library, read plays, and choose the one we think would be the most fun to do."

They selected a play that had many songs they loved to sing. They sold tickets to dozens of people and made money to be shared by all the company. Finally, on a Tuesday evening, they were ready, and it was time to raise the curtain.

The parents of the players were surprised and pleased with their children's acting. They made them promise to put on a show in the playhouse again before the month was over.

"What a good feeling it is to get so much praise," Sarah told her friends. "Now we can get busy preparing for the next show."

The Young Acting Company was a happy and cheerful group of boys and girls.

	Yes	No
1. Sarah and her friends wanted to be called the Young Acting Company.	○	○
2. Sarah had a brother Jack who was a good carpenter.	○	○
3. The children went to a bookstore to buy many books about plays.	○	○
4. The play the children selected had many songs the children loved to sing.	○	○
5. The parents of the children didn't want them to have an acting company.	○	○
6. The acting company was sad because no one praised the show.	○	○

2

People put their heads on it.

Sometimes it's small, and sometimes it's big.

It is always soft.

Some children toss it around when they're playing.

Is it — a cook
      — a cousin
      — a cushion

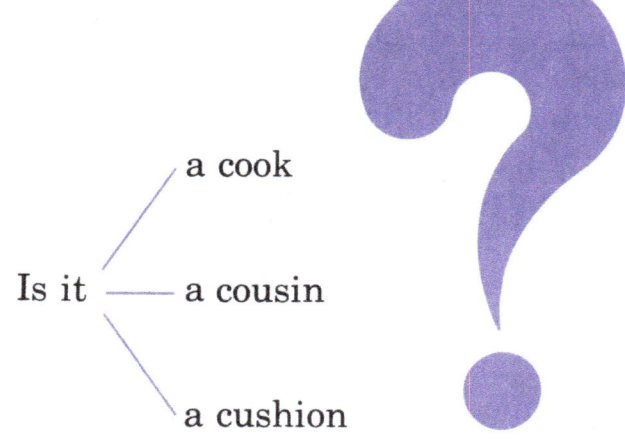

Almost every boy has one.

One boy throws it into the air, and another catches it with a glove.

It is used on a field called a diamond.

Is it — a breakfast
      — a baseball
      — a bookcase

Mother serves it with meat and potatoes.

If you eat it, it will help you grow strong.

It is always green.

Is it — screws
      — spinach
      — surprises

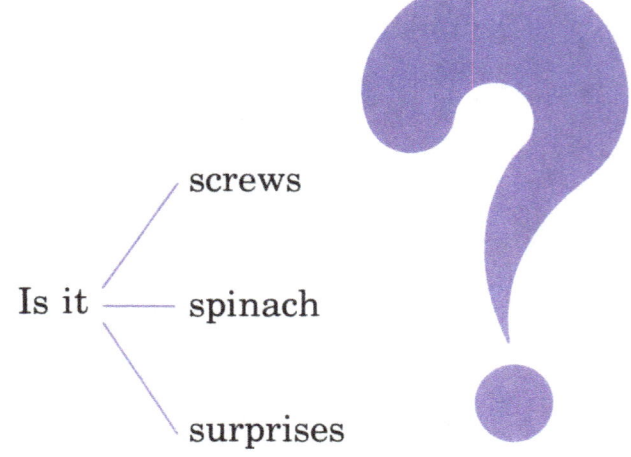

cent
center
celery
cereal
certain
circus
city
citizen
December
decide
bicycle
accident

face
lace
race
place
grace
space
palace

mice
nice
rice
price
slice
twice
advice
ice
police

dance
chance
since
prince
fence
ounce
bounce
announce
balance
distance
sentence
difference
pencil
once

piece
juice

cage
wage
age
huge
vegetable
change
strange
danger
large
orange

baggage
cabbage
cottage
village
package
sausage
voyage
carriage
college

gentle
general
giant
ginger
giraffe

magic
engine
engineer
pigeon

rough	ache	anger
tough	■	finger
enough	school	hunger
■	■	■
cough	character	angry
■		hungry
laugh		■
		jungle

edge	elephant	sugar
■	■	sure
bridge	telephone	
■	microphone	
porridge	xylophone	
■		
judge		

machine	measure
■	pleasure
parachute	

When Mother gives the grocer the money,

○ the grocer laughs at her vegetables.

○ she receives five cents in change.

○ the grocer begins to dance.

Adolph is handing Ralph a pencil that

○ accidentally pierced a hole in the book.

○ magically changed into a bicycle.

○ accidentally fell into a huge hole.

When the announcer speaks

○ her voice sounds angry.

○ she holds a large piece of celery.

○ she has a smile on her face.

The circus has come to town when

○ huge elephants come down the street.

○ the prince dances down the street.

○ mice ride bicycles down the street.

Mother accidentally

○ spilled orange juice on the tablecloth.

○ put sugar in the porridge.

○ put the telephone on the stove.

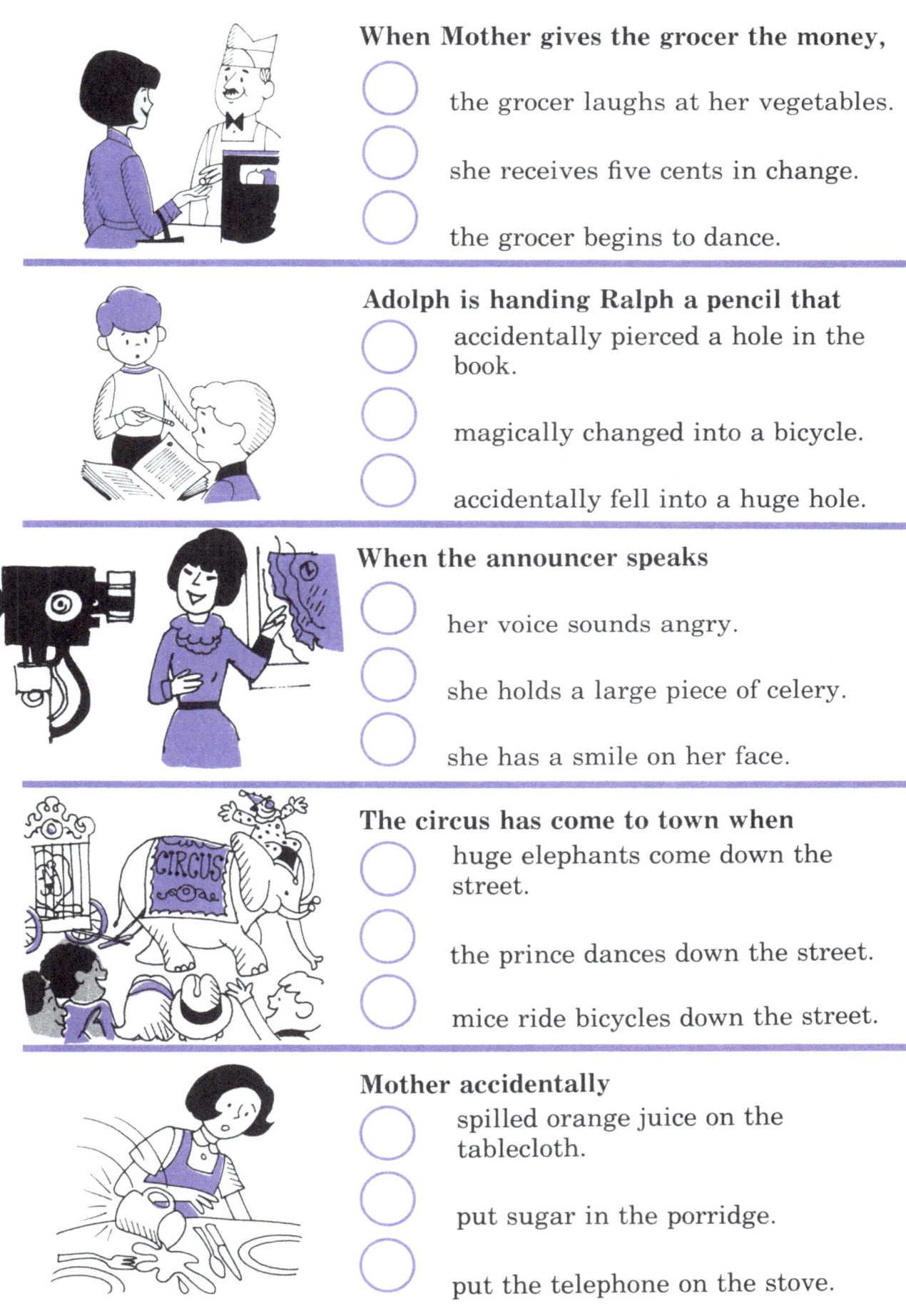

"Gee, Mom," said Grace, "this new cereal sure is good with sliced bananas. May I have another bowl of it and some more juice? This morning I'm very ——."

○ **hungry**   ○ **jungle**   ○ **huge**

After dinner our family enjoys sitting near our living-room fireplace. The flames seem to be gracefully ——.

○ **deciding**   ○ **dancing**   ○ **practicing**

"Wouldn't it be fun to have our own vegetable garden this summer?" said Marge.... "Yes," said her father. "That is a fine ——."

○ **suggestion**   ○ **silence**   ○ **slice**

My brother Bruce will start college this September. He has decided to study engineering. The school is a long distance from our home. Our family knows that Bruce is ——.

○ **electric**   ○ **excited**   ○ **exercising**

As Gene and Bruce Rivera stood near the edge of the bridge, they glanced all around them. "To the west," said Gene, "you'll be able to see the next ——."

○ **village**   ○ **voice**   ○ **vegetable**

You can skate and dance on ice.

Can you also dance on rice?

◯ Yes ◯ No

A giraffe can live in a circus cage.

Can it also draw on a page?

◯ Yes ◯ No

I can voyage to a strange place.

Can I voyage in outer space?

◯ Yes ◯ No

The sentence can be pronounced.

Can it also be announced?

◯ Yes ◯ No

A pencil can tear and pierce.

Can a pencil also be fierce?

◯ Yes ◯ No

A ruler can be fun and pleasure.

Can a ruler also measure?

◯ Yes ◯ No

An elephant's face feels rough.

Can its face also feel tough?

◯ Yes ◯ No

You notice pigeons at a glance.

Can you notice them at a dance?

◯ Yes ◯ No

3

Shall I tell you about the strange vegetables that can speak? Sometimes they even grow faces. I know you think that can't be so. But I know of one head of cabbage, one head of lettuce, and some celery that DO speak.

"I'm tall," said the celery. "And I can jump over the fence."

"I grow very large and round," said the cabbage. "I can be bounced like a ball."

"And I," said the lettuce, "grow graceful leaves."

You must agree, this was certainly a strange bunch of vegetables.

Put an X on the vegetable that bounces like a ball.

Our class took a trip to the zoo.

One of the funniest things I saw was a monkey being wheeled in a carriage.

I saw another monkey riding a tricycle.

In the large lion house we watched the giant jungle cats playing in their cages. They seemed tame. But our teacher told us not to get too close to the cages. She said the cats were fierce.

My favorite animal, however, is the elephant. He's so large — and yet he's so gentle.

Put an X on the favorite animal.

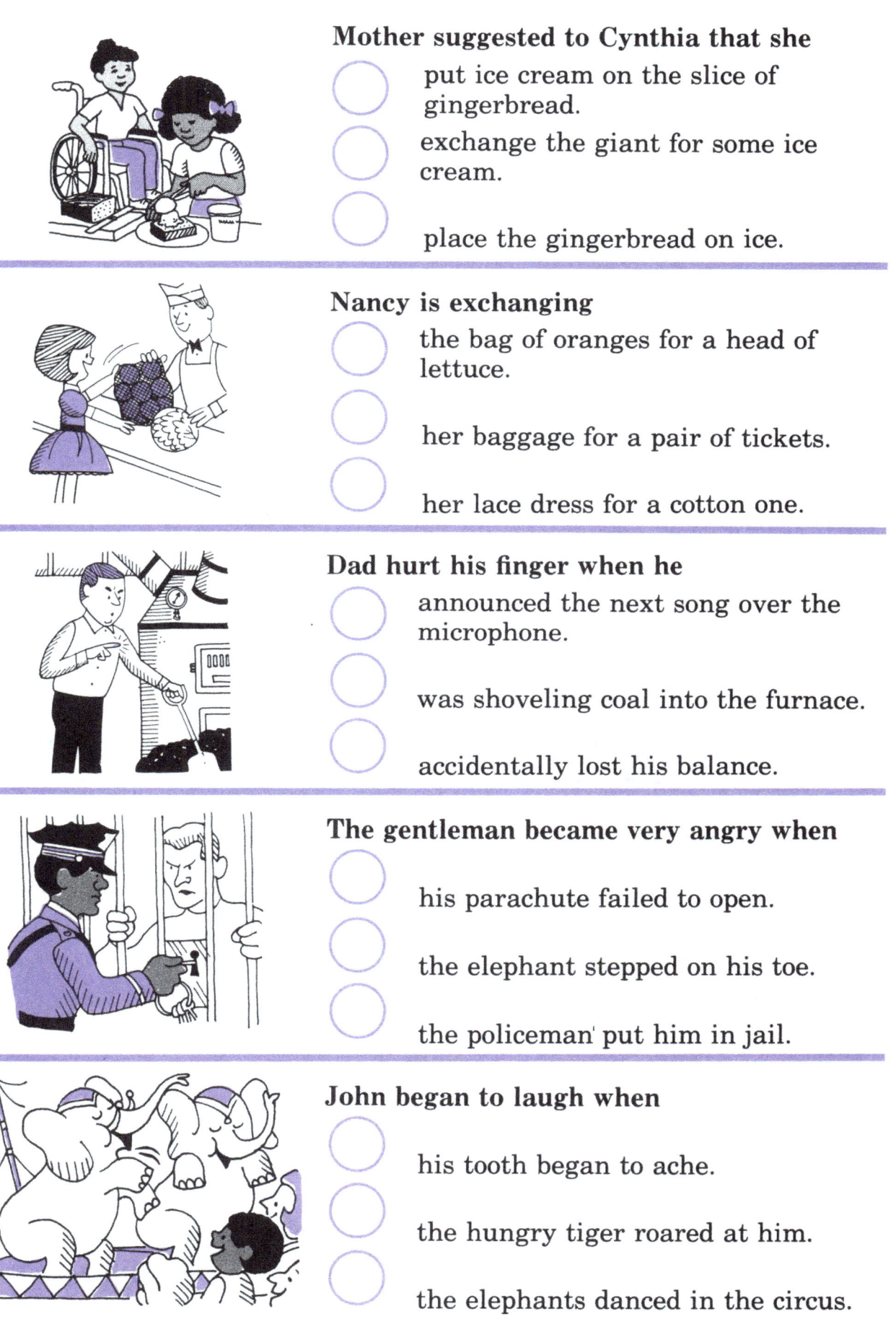

Mother suggested to Cynthia that she
- put ice cream on the slice of gingerbread.
- exchange the giant for some ice cream.
- place the gingerbread on ice.

Nancy is exchanging
- the bag of oranges for a head of lettuce.
- her baggage for a pair of tickets.
- her lace dress for a cotton one.

Dad hurt his finger when he
- announced the next song over the microphone.
- was shoveling coal into the furnace.
- accidentally lost his balance.

The gentleman became very angry when
- his parachute failed to open.
- the elephant stepped on his toe.
- the policeman put him in jail.

John began to laugh when
- his tooth began to ache.
- the hungry tiger roared at him.
- the elephants danced in the circus.

3

If you were a rabbit, maybe you would like to eat lettuce and ☐.

1. cabbage   2. cottage

If you want to keep milk cold, you would put it into a ☐.

1. telephone   2. refrigerator

There are many fierce animals living in the ☐.

1. jungle   2. garage

When the prince helps the princess into the carriage, he is being a ☐.

1. general   2. gentleman

One of the funniest and strangest things you can see at a circus is a monkey in a dress ☐.

1. dancing   2. danger

If you pull a pigeon out of a hat, you are performing ☐.

1. machine   2. magic

If you want to succeed as a dancer, you must be ☐.

1. general   2. graceful

To make the sound of his voice louder, an announcer speaks into a ☐.

1. microphone 2. xylophone

If a pilot decides to jump from her plane while it is flying, she must be wearing a ☐.

1. parachute   2. porridge

In our cellar we have a large ☐.

1. furnace   2. finger

Draw a line under anything that can cough.

a finger   a citizen

a policewoman   a voyage

cereal   some sugar

Draw a line under anything you could be when you grow up.

a bridge   a character

a voyage   a machine

a policeman   a policewoman

Draw a line under anything you could do with your sister.

dance   eat sugar

see a giant   go to school

be angry   run a race

Draw a line under anything that can dance.

a citizen   an engineer

a judge   a bounce

a fence   a sugar cube

Draw a line under anything you could ride on.

a village   December

a college   a bicycle

a giraffe   an orange

Draw a line under anything you would do if you were sick.

skate on ice   run a race

cough   fly in space

dance   join a circus

Draw a line under anything you would give as a gift.

ten cents   orange juice

some lace   a palace

a toothache   some danger

Draw a line under anything that is larger than a giraffe.

a giant   gingerbread

a palace   a carriage

a pencil   an elephant

Nancy raised her hand when the teacher asked who could read the sentences on page 3. "Some of the new words are hard to pronounce," said Nancy, "but I'll go home this afternoon and ———."

○ princess ○ practice ○ porridge

3

"I have to dance in the school play Tuesday," said Ralph. "Will you dance with me?" . . . "It's nice of you to ask me," said Angela. "It will certainly be a ———."

○ pleasure ○ measure ○ palace

The giraffe in the zoo noticed the children's strange remarks. "Just think, children," said the giraffe, "I don't have to stretch my neck to watch parades and look over ———."

○ rices ○ races ○ fences

Cynthia was sick in bed. Mother stood next to her with a teaspoon of medicine. "You'll have to take your medicine," she said. . . . "I don't like the taste of it," whispered Cynthia. "I wish it tasted like ———."

○ ice cream ○ nice dreams ○ a lace dress

Cecilia was excited. She was firing a rocket. "It will be strange and dangerous," she said. "This device will pierce the far distances of outer ———."

○ city ○ slice ○ space

You could welcome a stranger.

> Should you also welcome danger?

○ Yes   ○ No

A giant could eat a sardine.

> Should he also drink gasoline?

○ Yes   ○ No

Mice have noses on their faces.

> Do they also have sailboat races?

○ Yes   ○ No

An angry elephant may charge.

> Would a hungry elephant also be large?

○ Yes   ○ No

A pigeon can sit on a hedge.

> Can it also sit on an edge?

○ Yes   ○ No

A rocket can fly into space.

> Can it also fly into lace?

○ Yes   ○ No

You can carry baggage on a train.

> Can you carry a package in the rain?

○ Yes   ○ No

You can eat cabbage in a dream.

> Can you also eat sausage in ice cream?

○ Yes   ○ No

3

The circus came to our city, and my friends and I were lucky enough to go.

We watched as a tall man performed magic.

"Ladies and gentlemen," shouted the man, "if you will watch closely, I'll change this huge package into a fair and graceful princess!"

He placed his finger on the package, and suddenly there was a large puff of smoke.

There stood the princess.

Put an X on the man who can change a package into a princess.

Mr. Lacey owns the drugstore in the center of our town.

Besides selling chocolates and ice cream, Mr. Lacey has cough medicine for people with colds. He also prepares other medicine for people who need it.

Many of our town's citizens go to him for advice.

Put an X on the person who prepares medicine for sick people.

There are twelve months in the year. After November comes the month of ☐.

1. Thursday   2. December

Sticking your finger into a lion's cage is ☐.

1. dangerous   2. difference

If your friend moves to another city, you can call him on the ☐.

1. telephone   2. xylophone

Before we had electric refrigerators, many people kept their food in ☐.

1. an icebox   2. a fireplace

On cold December mornings many children eat a nice bowl of hot ☐.

1. cereal   2. celery

On cold, icy days many men put their cars in a ☐.

1. garage   2. grocery

If a train stops suddenly, the engineer may check for trouble in the ☐.

1. exchange   2. engine

You may not be able to do your lessons in school if you don't have a ☐.

1. pencil   2. palace

One place that's closed on some holidays is the school ☐.

1. orange   2. office

If you are away from home for a long time, you may need a lot of ☐.

1. baggage   2. cabbage

3

63

Susan's father was ill. He had a bad cough. He asked Susan to buy him some groceries.

"Would you ask the grocer for the vegetables and fruit on this list? Be sure to remember the lettuce and oranges for dinner." "May I choose my own cereal, dad?" asked Susan.

Certainly," said her father, "and you may choose some ice cream, too. If the packages are too heavy for you, ask the grocer to deliver them."

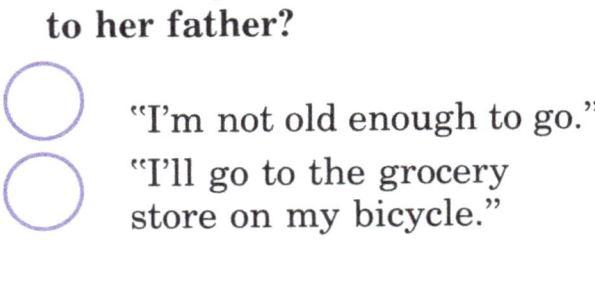

1. What do you think Susan said to her father?
   ○ "I'm not old enough to go."
   ○ "I'll go to the grocery store on my bicycle."

2. What do you think Susan did?
   ○ She rode her bicycle to the grocery and shopped.
   ○ She rode her tricycle over the bridge and hopped.

3. What do you think the grocer said to Susan?
   ○ "Sure, I have this medicine."
   ○ "Your father is certainly lucky to have your help."

I was just four years old when my father took me and my sister Grace to our first circus.

That day I saw a monkey ride a bicycle and an elephant do a graceful dance. I saw seals balance balls on their tiny noses. I wanted to pet the lions, but my father said no. They were dangerous.

It all looked like magic to me. I looked at everything with such a surprised expression that my father laughed at me and Grace said I was silly.

1. What do you think Grace asked?
   ○ "When can we see another circus?"
   ○ "When can we go home to the jungle?"

2. What do you think Father said?
   ○ "I'll buy you your very own elephant."
   ○ "We'll come to the circus again next year."

3. What do you think I asked?
   ○ "Do the elephants sleep in cages?"
   ○ "Do the giraffes eat parachutes?"

Draw a line under anything you could find in a doctor's office.

a pigeon	a microphone
a scale	a telephone
a prince	cough medicine

Draw a line under anything that you can slice.

an orange	celery
a xylophone	gingerbread
cereal	sugar

Draw a line under anything you can find in a jungle.

a tricycle	huge animals
elephants	giraffes
a village	a parachute

Draw a line under anything that runs by electricity.

a refrigerator	an engine
a fireplace	a machine
a bicycle	a microphone

Draw a line under anything you can see in a circus.

an elephant	a fierce lion
a city	an announcer
a giant	a schoolroom

Draw a line under anything you can find in a schoolroom.

a red pencil	a sentence
a sausage	a tape measure
a garage	pages in a book

Draw a line under anything you can buy in a grocery.

celery	a giraffe
medicine	sugar
vegetables	lettuce

Draw a line under anything that gives you pleasure.

dancing	seeing a circus
bicycling	coughing
being hungry	a toothache

3

65

What's the story about?

Once, as Riccardo was out riding his bicycle, there was a loud crash behind him. When he glanced back, he saw an awful automobile accident. He noticed that glass was broken and that the men in the cars seemed to be hurt. He ran to help them, since he could see that a piece of glass had cut one man's face. The other man's fingers were cut.

"I should call a policeman," said Riccardo. "These men need hospital care."

When help came, the men were taken care of properly, and their cars were taken to a garage for repairs. Riccardo was praised for being a useful and helpful citizen.

○ Riccardo's Strange Voyage

○ A Policeman Comes to Help

○ Riccardo is a Helpful Citizen

One of the things that Ken and Nancy liked most about school was the cooking class on Mondays.

On a Monday in December their teacher announced that the class would bake a huge gingerbread man. She told them how many eggs to use and how much flour and sugar to add.

When he had been baked long enough, they took him out of the oven to cool.

After they had taken the man out of the oven, the children had to decide what to do with him.

They got so much pleasure from cooking the gingerbread man that they couldn't decide what to do with him. Should they slice him so that each person would receive a piece? Or should they save him?

○ Baking a Gingerbread Man

○ A Decision about Cooking

○ A Magic Gingerbread Man

The wild elephants and lions in the ☐ hunt for food when they are ☐.

1. jungle   2. hungry

When we shopped at the grocery, we asked the grocer to pick out a ☐ head of ☐ for us.

1. lettuce   2. large

When the ☐ in the circus noticed that the dancers were ready, he stepped up to the ☐.

1. announcer   2. microphone

Ralph chopped ☐ to use in the ☐ he was making.

1. sausage   2. soup

There's a big ☐ between ☐ weather and August weather.

1. difference   2. December

Bruce was ☐ that Cindy would enjoy a bowl of ☐ if she put some sliced fruit on it.

1. cereal   2. certain

Ms. Moss received a prize for being a good ☐ of our ☐.

1. citizen   2. city

If your new skirt is not long ☐, you can ☐ it for a larger size.

1. enough   2. exchange

If you accidentally drop a ☐ of glasses, they may break into many ☐.

1. pieces   2. package

The monkey got ☐ up in the branches of a tree in the ☐.

1. jungle   2. tangled

Draw a line under anything you may do without asking Mother.

go to college	go to the moon
eat cabbage	bounce a ball
laugh	phone a pal

Draw a line under anything you can do in five minutes.

draw a face	make a machine
slice bread	eat an orange
eat cereal	go to France

Draw a line under anything you can do with your father.

eat rice	ride a giraffe
run a race	be a general
dance	be a gentleman

Draw a line under anything you can bring home.

a badge	an elephant
sugar cookies	a giant
a princess	a telephone

Draw a line under anything you can have a race with.

an elephant	a jungle
a laugh	a strange
a bicycle	a judge

Draw a line under anything you can keep in a cage.

vegetables	mice
sentences	pigeons
a giraffe	an ache

Draw a line under anything you can put in a package.

a school	a jungle
an orange	a parachute
a general	sugar

Draw a line under anything you can slice.

a cough	cabbage
vegetables	sausage
a machine	a bridge

What's the story about?

Ever since Madge was a little girl, she had dreamed that one day she would go to college and become a great engineer. Each day she could scarcely wait to race down to the bridge that crossed the river.

"One day I will build a huge bridge that will cross a large river," said Madge. "Perhaps I will have my own office in a big city too. When I succeed, all the ladies and gentlemen will ask my advice, and I will gladly give it."

It was nice to think ahead, and exciting to make so many plans.

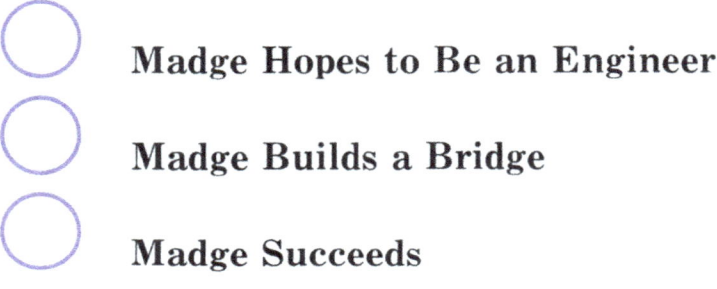

○ Madge Hopes to Be an Engineer

○ Madge Builds a Bridge

○ Madge Succeeds

Wouldn't it be strange if all animals could speak to each other the way we do? If we pretend hard enough, we can surely hear our circus friends, the elephant and the giraffe, having an interesting talk.

"Isn't it nice to know that we bring pleasure and excitement to so many children who come to watch us at the circus?" said the giraffe to the elephant. "Even I cheer when Miss Starr gracefully balances a saucer on the end of your trunk. Such a great act must have taken months of hard practice."

"Yes," said the elephant, "but when I glance around the circus tent and notice the happy faces of all the children, I know it was worth it."

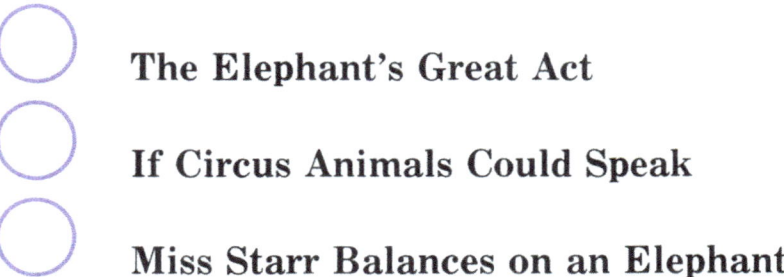

○ The Elephant's Great Act

○ If Circus Animals Could Speak

○ Miss Starr Balances on an Elephant

3

If you wanted to have fun outdoors

If you wanted to have fun outdoors, what would you do?

○ practice baseball

○ carry garbage out

○ slice vegetables

If you wanted to have fun outdoors, where would you go?

○ to the refrigerator

○ to a beach cottage

○ to a schoolroom

If you wanted to have fun outdoors, what could you do in the sky?

○ ride a bicycle

○ visit a village

○ make a parachute jump

If you wanted to have fun indoors

If you wanted to have fun indoors, what would you do?

○ get a toothache

○ draw with colored pencils

○ go to Philadelphia

If you wanted to have fun indoors, where would you have it?

○ in a hot furnace

○ in a circus tent

○ in a strange jungle

If you wanted to have fun indoors at home, what would you do?

○ play the xylophone

○ hurt your finger

○ carry garbage out

Princess Karen's Magic Dream

Karen read many tales about princes and princesses. Sometimes she pretended that she was a princess with magic powers.

"I'll close my eyes and travel a great distance to our huge white palace," she said. She began to daydream.

When Karen imagined herself at the palace, she noticed that the prince was unhappy.

"We're in great danger, Karen," said the prince. "The giant has said that he'll destroy our city. He is tough and fierce, and I'm not sure I can stop him."

"I have magic powers, Prince," said Karen. "I'll surely think of something that will forever destroy this dangerous giant."

Sure enough, just as the prince had feared, the giant appeared the next day. He was larger than Karen had expected.

Just as he was about to destroy the palace, Karen cast a magic spell, and he changed into stone.

The people cheered with excitement. The giant would never again harm their village.

The prince was so happy that he announced that there would be a dance at the palace that evening and everyone could come.

The prince and Karen danced gracefully in the center of the floor.

Suddenly Princess Karen remembered that this was all a dream, so she stepped into the golden carriage for her trip home.

Karen smiled happily, for even if all that had happened was not true, it had been a nice dream.

	Yes	No
1. Karen cast a magic spell.	○	○
2. The prince was angry because Karen used her magic powers.	○	○
3. The giant was huge and fierce and wanted to destroy the prince's city.	○	○
4. Princess Karen used a magic spell to turn the giant into an elephant.	○	○
5. After the giant was destroyed, the prince invited everyone to a dance at the palace.	○	○
6. Karen was a real princess who lived in the prince's palace.	○	○

3

It is a large animal.

It has a thick, rough hide.

It lifts food with its huge trunk.

Sometimes it is trained to dance in a circus.

Is it — an elephant / an aquarium / an engineer

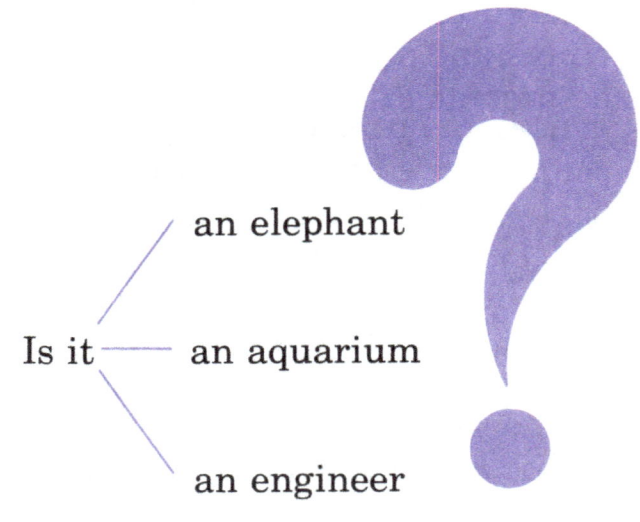

Some refrigerators won't work without it.

It can be dangerous.

It makes many engines and machines work.

Is it — exercise / electricity / excitement

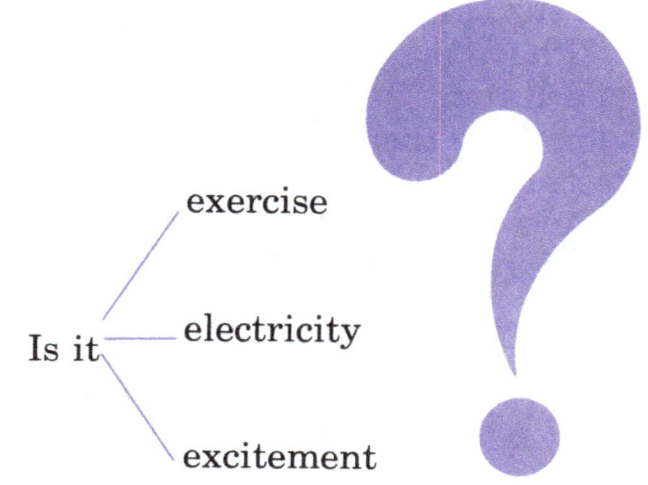

My job is to protect the people of the city.

If an accident happens, I am called to help.

I help children at school crossings.

Am I — a pigeon / a parachute / a policeman

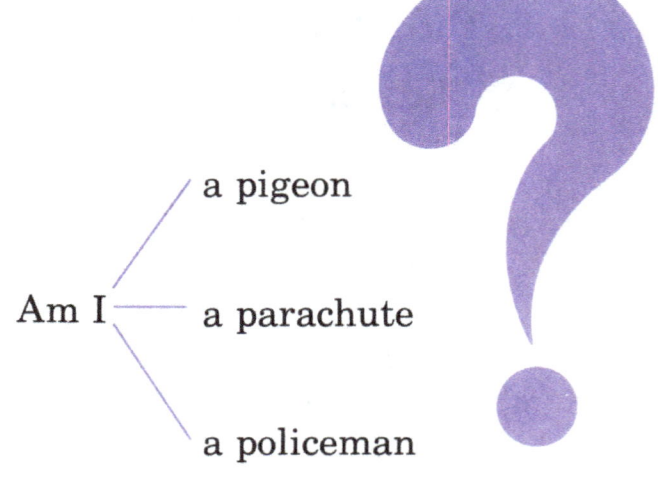

An Exciting Jump

Vince and his parents were on their way to the circus. When they arrived, Vince noticed a large crowd around the parachute jump. He said that he would like a chance to jump. When his parents were sure that it was safe, they agreed to let him try.

First Vince was lifted onto a platform. He watched with excitement as the parachute was strapped onto him. It seemed like a huge pack, and was made of strong material. He made sure that the lines were not tangled.

At last it was time to jump. Vince moved to the edge of the platform and glanced down. The ground seemed to be a great distance down, but he took a big step and opened his parachute, and soon he was floating gracefully in space.

Suddenly a voice said something. He turned, and, sure enough, a pigeon was speaking to him.

"You're a very brave boy, Vince. I've decided to fly along with you and protect you all the way down. I've had many years of practice at this sort of thing, but this is your first parachute jump."

"Thank you, pigeon, for being my friend," said Vince.

Once Vince reached the ground, his parents welcomed him warmly. He told of his strange pigeon friend in space, but when he glanced at his parents' faces, he decided that they didn't believe him. Would you?

	Yes	No
1. Vince and his parents went to visit a village in the center of a jungle.	○	○
2. Vince was excited about his chance to jump over a fence.	○	○
3. The parachute was strapped onto Vince as he stood on a platform.	○	○
4. As Vince floated in space, something spoke to him.	○	○
5. A policeman decided to fly along with Vince to protect him.	○	○
6. Vince told his parents about the strange pigeon, and they believed him.	○	○

3

It grows in the South and is shipped to grocers everywhere.

It is juicy, and when it's squeezed it gives lots of juice.

It can also be sliced and used in a salad.

Is it —— an office / an orange / an engine ?

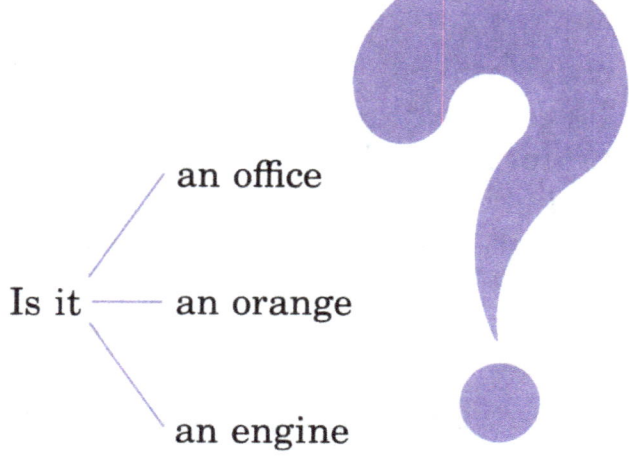

It is in the refrigerator at the grocery.

Sometimes after you have cereal at breakfast, you eat it with eggs.

It can be sliced from a large piece of meat.

Is it —— space / sausage / spinach ?

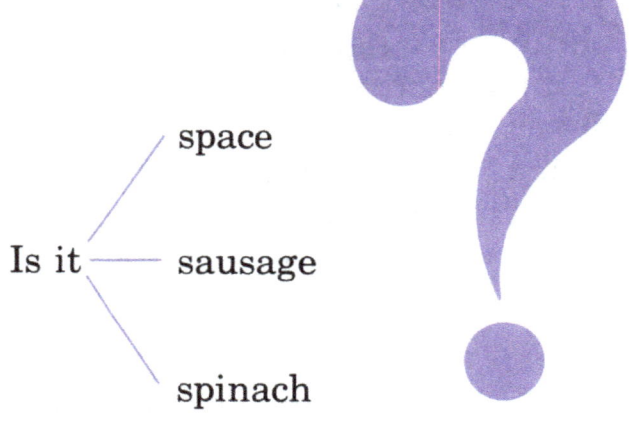

You can place a cup in the center of it.

Sometimes your kitten drinks milk from it.

If you drop it, it may break.

Is it —— a saucer / a sauce / a saucepan ?

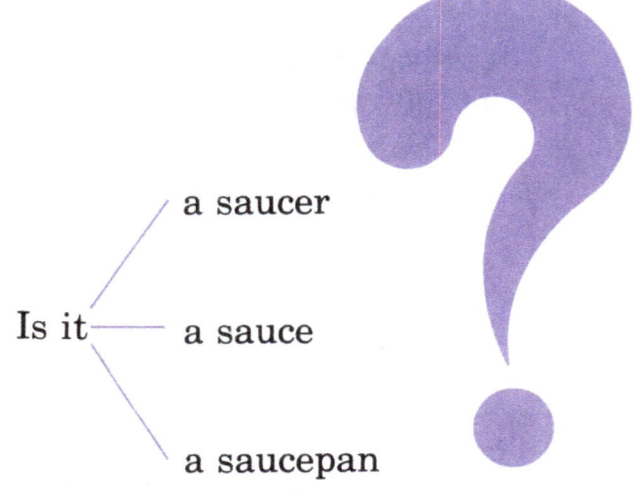

74

bought fought brought ■ caught taught ■ daughter ■ naughty	weigh sleigh ■ neighbor ■ eight ■ eighty ■ eighth	high ■ fight light might night right sight tight bright fright ■ straight	bough ■ though ■ through

4

calf half ■ salmon ■ walk talk stalk chalk ■ yolk	lamb ■ limb ■ comb ■ crumb thumb ■ climb	knee ■ knew ■ knife ■ knock ■ know ■ known	often soften ■ fasten ■ listen ■ castle ■ whistle ■ Christmas ■ chestnut

75

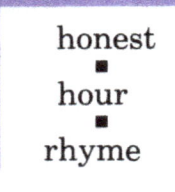

- honest
- hour
- rhyme

- Wednesday
- handsome
- handkerchief

- scene
- scissors

- wrap
- wren
- write
- wrote
- whole
- whose
- two
- sword
- toward
- answer

- cupboard
- raspberry

- island

- autumn

- pasture
- picture
- furniture
- nature

- action
- nation
- station
- attention
- direction

- soldier

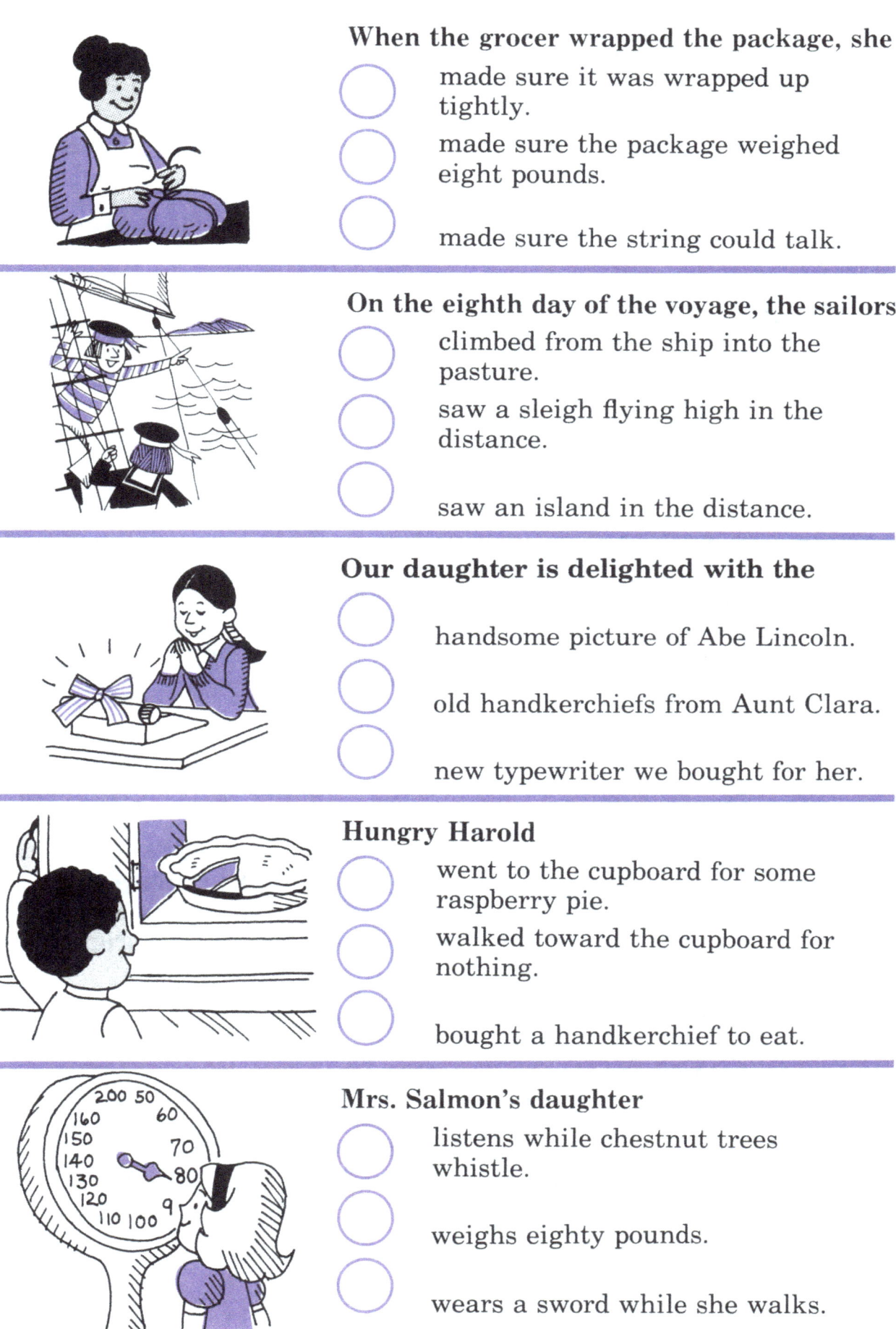

When the grocer wrapped the package, she
- made sure it was wrapped up tightly.
- made sure the package weighed eight pounds.
- made sure the string could talk.

On the eighth day of the voyage, the sailors
- climbed from the ship into the pasture.
- saw a sleigh flying high in the distance.
- saw an island in the distance.

Our daughter is delighted with the
- handsome picture of Abe Lincoln.
- old handkerchiefs from Aunt Clara.
- new typewriter we bought for her.

Hungry Harold
- went to the cupboard for some raspberry pie.
- walked toward the cupboard for nothing.
- bought a handkerchief to eat.

Mrs. Salmon's daughter
- listens while chestnut trees whistle.
- weighs eighty pounds.
- wears a sword while she walks.

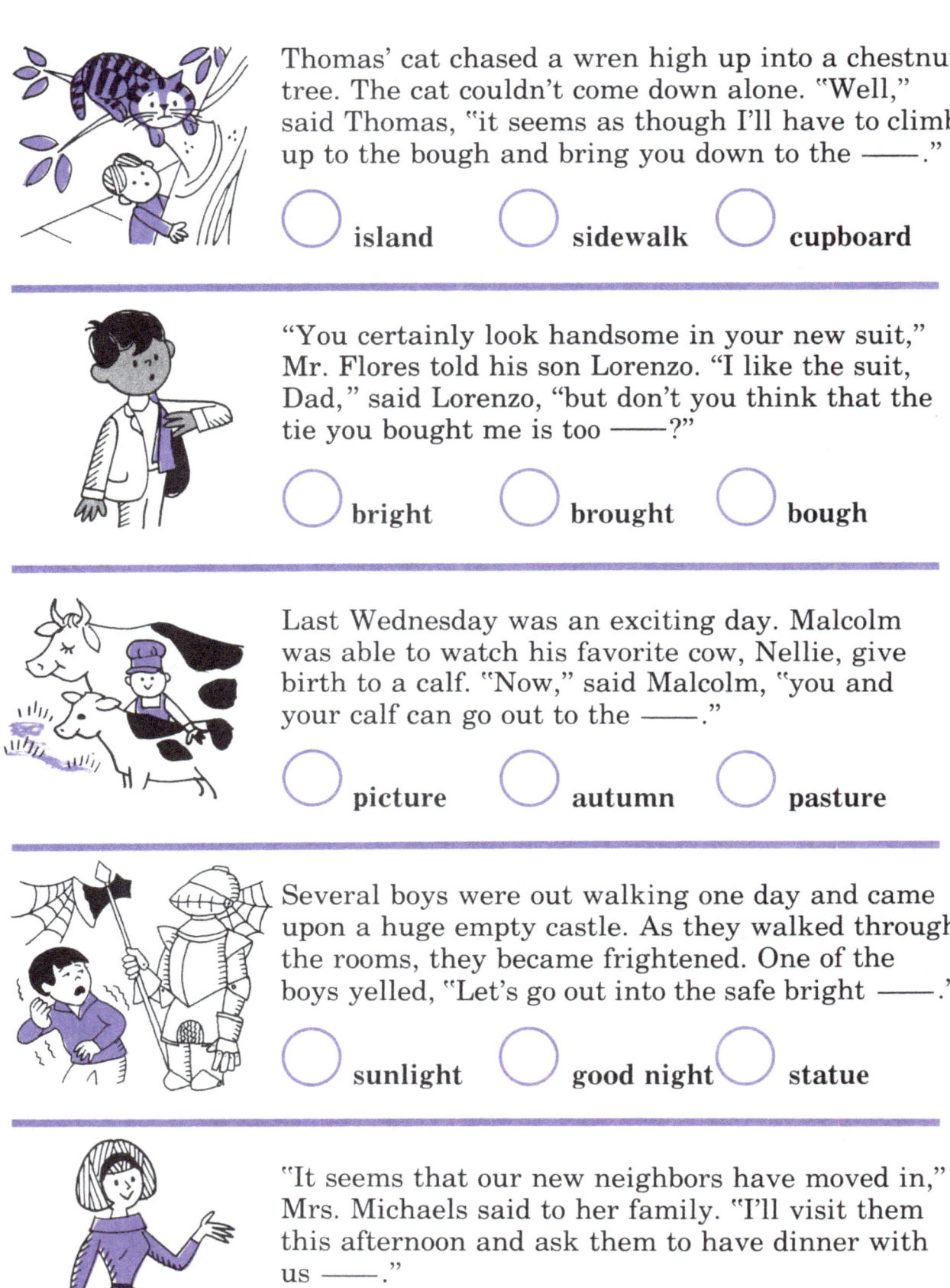

Thomas' cat chased a wren high up into a chestnut tree. The cat couldn't come down alone. "Well," said Thomas, "it seems as though I'll have to climb up to the bough and bring you down to the ———."

○ island   ○ sidewalk   ○ cupboard

"You certainly look handsome in your new suit," Mr. Flores told his son Lorenzo. "I like the suit, Dad," said Lorenzo, "but don't you think that the tie you bought me is too ———?"

○ bright   ○ brought   ○ bough

Last Wednesday was an exciting day. Malcolm was able to watch his favorite cow, Nellie, give birth to a calf. "Now," said Malcolm, "you and your calf can go out to the ———."

○ picture   ○ autumn   ○ pasture

Several boys were out walking one day and came upon a huge empty castle. As they walked through the rooms, they became frightened. One of the boys yelled, "Let's go out into the safe bright ———."

○ sunlight   ○ good night   ○ statue

"It seems that our new neighbors have moved in," Mrs. Michaels said to her family. "I'll visit them this afternoon and ask them to have dinner with us ———."

○ through   ○ tonight   ○ upward

A cold might make you sneeze.

   Can a cold make a squeeze?

   ◯ Yes   ◯ No

A typewriter keeps lines straight.

   Can a typewriter count to eight?

   ◯ Yes   ◯ No

Answers can be taught.

   Can answers also be caught?

   ◯ Yes   ◯ No

Hugh can use his knees to climb.

   Can he use his knees to rhyme?

   ◯ Yes   ◯ No

You can hold a pencil lightly.

   Can you hold a pencil tightly?

   ◯ Yes   ◯ No

A whistle can be bought.

   Can a whistle also be taught?

   ◯ Yes   ◯ No

A scale is often used to weigh.

   Can a scale guide a sleigh?

   ◯ Yes   ◯ No

A clown can be delightful.

   Can a clown be frightful?

   ◯ Yes   ◯ No

4

Tom and Lorna thought it might be fun to make a birdhouse for their chestnut tree. They bought the wood from the village merchant and brought it home.

When they finished the birdhouse, they hunted for a straight, strong tree limb. They knew that the house would have to be fastened tightly or a storm could knock it down.

Tom climbed the tree and wrapped strong wire round the limb and ran it through the birdhouse. Not long after they finished, a tiny wren flew into the birdhouse.

Put an X on the thing that found a home.

Maria and her family lived on a farm. It was Maria's job to take care of the lambs.

The lambs were so fond of Maria that they walked along with her even when she visited the neighbors.

Once a year, Maria and her father used shearing scissors to cut the lambs' wool. They weighed and packaged the wool to sell to a merchant in the city.

Maria loved her lambs and thought of them as her friends.

Put an X on the thing that Maria used in helping her father.

Alice Crumb hurt her arm, so she

○ couldn't write with her right hand.

○ couldn't walk or talk.

○ couldn't watch TV.

Carol drew a straight line

○ through the sentence she had written.

○ to make a border around her picture.

○ with her comb and brush.

Lawrence noticed a bright, shiny

○ egg yolk in the pasture.

○ penny on the sidewalk.

○ penny on an island.

For his birthday, Carlos is receiving a

○ set of books.

○ box of handkerchiefs and a warm scarf for winter.

○ picture of a castle on an island.

Mother went to the cupboard to

○ find it as bare as a desert.

○ get a knife to cut the raspberry pie.

○ weigh the cake she had made.

4

81

To put out a fire, firemen fasten their hoses to a fire ☐.

1. hydrant   2. guide

When an egg is cracked open, you can see the round yellow center that is called the ☐.

1. walk   2. yolk

If you take a test in school, you want to give the right ☐.

1. answers   2. swords

It is thoughtful to bring a cake to your new next-door ☐.

1. sleigh   2. neighbor

Wrens will come to your lawn if you feed them ☐.

1. calves   2. crumbs

If you are asked to write on the chalkboard, you will have to get a piece of ☐.

1. chalk   2. calf

When Mother brings home the groceries she has bought, she puts them in the ☐.

1. chestnut   2. cupboard

If you see a very funny picture, you don't cry; you ☐.

1. laugh   2. listen

If you used chalk to write on your neighbor's sidewalk, you would be ☐.

1. naughty   2. lightly

If you wanted to cut out a picture for your scrapbook, you would use a pair of ☐.

1. swords   2. scissors

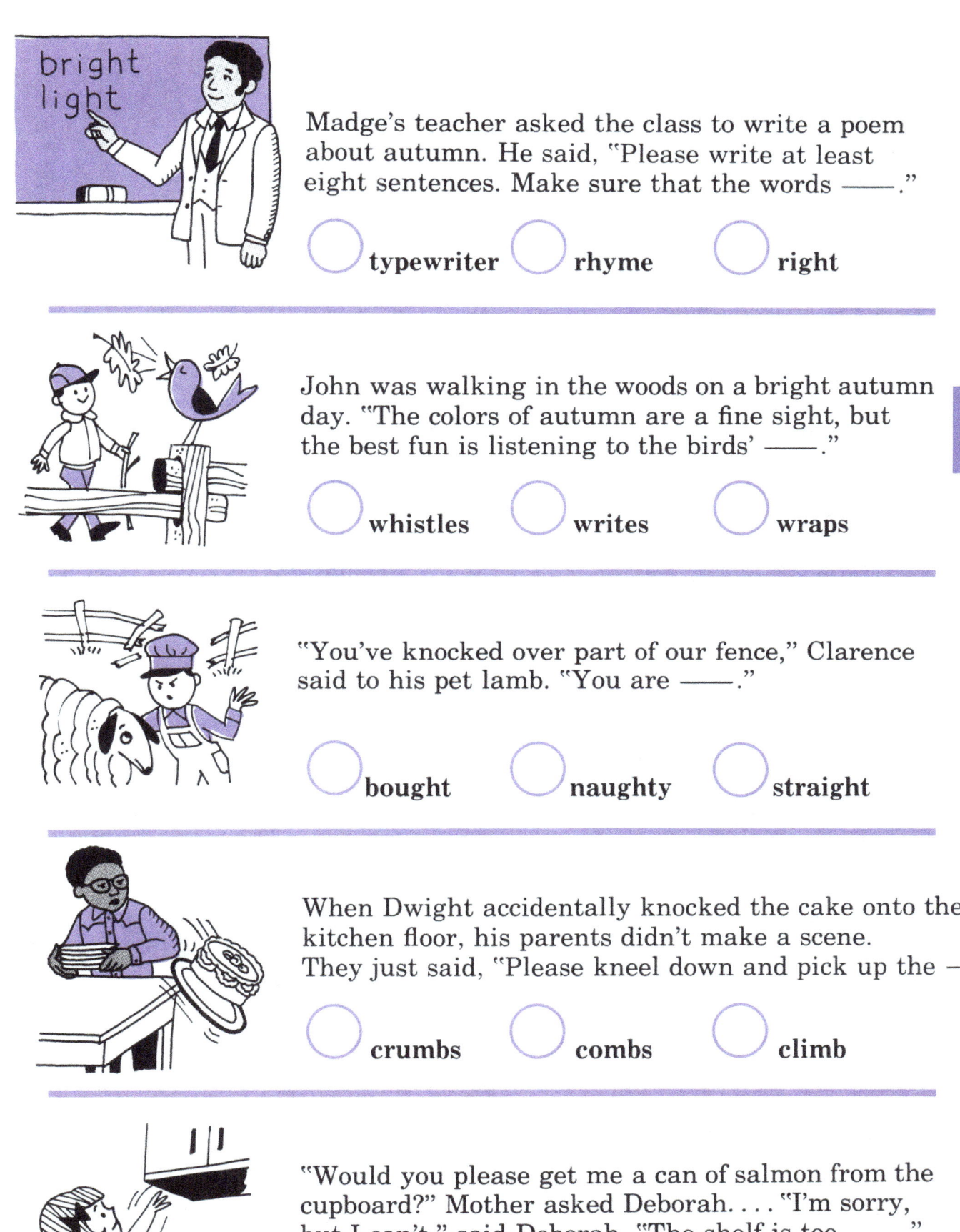

Madge's teacher asked the class to write a poem about autumn. He said, "Please write at least eight sentences. Make sure that the words ——."

○ typewriter ○ rhyme ○ right

John was walking in the woods on a bright autumn day. "The colors of autumn are a fine sight, but the best fun is listening to the birds' ——."

○ whistles ○ writes ○ wraps

"You've knocked over part of our fence," Clarence said to his pet lamb. "You are ——."

○ bought ○ naughty ○ straight

When Dwight accidentally knocked the cake onto the kitchen floor, his parents didn't make a scene. They just said, "Please kneel down and pick up the ——."

○ crumbs ○ combs ○ climb

"Would you please get me a can of salmon from the cupboard?" Mother asked Deborah. . . . "I'm sorry, but I can't," said Deborah. "The shelf is too ——."

○ honest ○ high ○ handsome

83

4

You can be president of a nation.

　Can you also be president of a station?

　　◯ **Yes**　　◯ **No**

I can clean up my crumbs.

　Can I also clean up my thumbs?

　　◯ **Yes**　　◯ **No**

If a sleigh can be bought,

　can a sleigh be brought?

　　◯ **Yes**　　◯ **No**

You can give me a calf.

　Can you also give me a laugh?

　　◯ **Yes**　　◯ **No**

A lamb can be caught.

　Can a lamb also be taught?

　　◯ **Yes**　　◯ **No**

Betsy dances lightly on her toes.

　Can she also dance nightly on her nose?

　　◯ **Yes**　　◯ **No**

You can paint a lovely scene.

　Can you paint a screen green?

　　◯ **Yes**　　◯ **No**

You can knock on a castle door.

　Can you also knock on the castle floor?

　　◯ **Yes**　　◯ **No**

Every autumn the Alvarez family brings its circus to our city. Almost overnight, an empty lot becomes a magic city of tents, animals, and exciting acts. It is quite a sight.

You can see a man swallow a sword.

You can also see the knife thrower fling a knife through the air.

The tightrope walker kneeling and balancing on the high wire is also delightful to watch.

No matter how often you go to the Alvarez's circus, you'll be sure to enjoy it.

Put an X on the thing someone flings.

4

"Wouldn't it be fun to make our own Christmas gifts this year?" Jane said to her sister. "We have many pieces of bright cloth. We could cut them into squares for handkerchiefs."

Jane cut each piece with her scissors. Her sister then sewed a straight hem on each one.

They fastened lace on the edges to make the handkerchiefs even nicer.

The sisters then wrapped each gift tightly with gaily colored paper.

Put an X on Jane.

85

4

If you listen carefully, you might hear the wind ☐.

1. whistle   2. thistle

When winter comes and there is lots of snow, your neighbors might go for a ride in a ☐.

1. sleigh   2. stalk

If you walk around a farm, you might see many calves and cows eating grass in the ☐.

1. picture   2. pasture

If your mother has to tighten her bicycle handlebars, she may need a ☐.

1. wrench   2. wreath

After I wash the clothes, I will hang them in the bright sunlight on a ☐.

1. clothesline   2. cupboard

If you try to climb a tree, you might slip and hurt your ☐.

1. lamb   2. thumb

If you want to keep your hair neat, you should use a brush and a ☐.

1. comb   2. crumb

If you were a prince or a princess, you might live in a ☐.

1. castle   2. chestnut

If you have six handkerchiefs and receive two more, you will have ☐.

1. eighty   2. eight

If you aren't left-handed, you write with your ☐ hand.

1. right   2. whole

Sandy was babysitting with her neighbor's daughter, Linda. While Sandy was reading, Linda slipped out of sight. Sandy heard a loud crash in the kitchen. She caught Linda kneeling on the table and reaching into the cupboard. A broken jar of raspberry jam lay next to her.

"I didn't mean to knock it down, but I thought I'd have some raspberry jam," said Linda.

"You should have asked me for the jam," said Sandy. "You were naughty to try to get it yourself."

1. What else might Sandy say?
   - "You're too honest to eat raspberry jam."
   - "The cupboard is too high for you to reach."

2. What do you think Linda said to Sandy?
   - "I only wanted a doughnut."
   - "You're right. I knew the cupboard was too high."

3. What do you think Linda did?
   - She climbed down and ran to comb her hair.
   - She climbed down and cleaned up the whole mess.

Grandpa Wright was eighty years old Wednesday, and Mother planned a big party for him.

"I baked Grandpa's favorite crumb cake for him to have tonight," Mother said on Wednesday morning.

Our whole family brought nicely wrapped gifts for Grandpa. When he walked through the door, we all clapped and cheered. His eyes had tears in them. He certainly was delighted.

1. What do you think Grandpa said?
   - "How thoughtful of you!"
   - "I don't often whistle at night."

2. What did the family and Grandpa Wright do?
   - They thought about autumn.
   - They talked and laughed till late at night.

3. What do you think Mother said after the party?
   - "I'm glad we had the party on Thursday."
   - "Grandpa was delighted with the party."

Draw a line under anything you can weigh.

a castle	raspberries
a salmon	firelight
a knee	a lamb

Draw a line under anything you might find in a kitchen cupboard.

raspberry jam	a box of crumbs
salmon	an autumn day
a laugh	a box of combs

Draw a line under anything you can wrap in a package.

a pasture	handkerchiefs
furniture	a nightgown
a picture	a box of chalk

Draw a line under anything you can listen to as you walk.

a yolk	the sunlight
a picture	a typewriter
a wren	a whistle

Draw a line under anything that can talk.

a daughter	a soldier
a crumb	a light
a wren	a picture

Draw a line under anything that can be straight.

a comb	chalk
a raspberry	a clothesline
scissors	a chestnut

Draw a line under anything that you can cut in half with scissors.

a comb	writing paper
a knife	handkerchiefs
a picture	a castle

Draw a line under anything that might make you laugh.

an egg yolk	a silly rhyme
a typewriter	a straight line
a chestnut	a naughty calf

What's the story about?

Linda's parents were talking one day and her mother said, "Wouldn't it be nice if we bought Linda a typewriter as a gift for her birthday?"

"Yes," agreed her father. "We can go to the store tonight and pick one out."

The following day, while Linda was out playing on the sidewalk, the deliveryman brought a package to her door.

"This is a gift for you, Linda," said her mother.

When Linda ripped open the wrapping, she was delighted with the typewriter.

Her mother taught her how to use it, and Linda practiced the typing exercises every day.

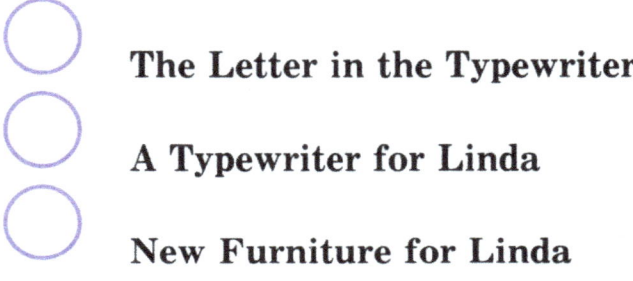

○ The Letter in the Typewriter

○ A Typewriter for Linda

○ New Furniture for Linda

When autumn comes, our whole family enjoys walking in the nearby park. The handsome trees have colorful leaves. We often meet our neighbor Mrs. Rice and her two daughters walking and enjoying the warm sunlight.

One day Mother said, "If you listen carefully, you'll hear the wind whistling through the trees. It sounds like a song."

"Yes," we all answered, "you're right, Mother. It does."

"Let's all make up some rhymes to sing along with the sounds of autumn," said Mother.

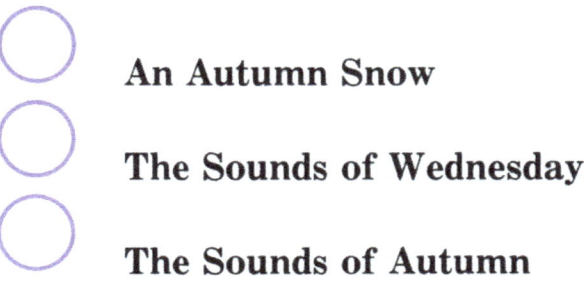

○ An Autumn Snow

○ The Sounds of Wednesday

○ The Sounds of Autumn

Jane painted a picture of a fishing ☐ as her father fished for ☐.

1. salmon   2. scene

As Carol ☐ to pick up her handkerchief, she fell and hurt her right ☐.

1. knee   2. knelt

4

Thomas ☐ how sharp the ☐ was, so he put it away in a safe place.

1. knew   2. knife

When John saw his ☐ friends, he quickly walked ☐ them.

1. toward   2. two

Father invited our ☐ children to go for a ride in our ☐.

1. sleigh   2. neighbors'

The ☐ that Clara was writing with broke in ☐.

1. half   2. chalk

Some people have good ☐ and can see well at ☐.

1. night   2. eyesight

Mrs. Houghton ☐ a new nightgown for her ☐.

1. daughter   2. bought

Mother ☐ ☐ her skin by putting on hand lotion.

1. often   2. softens

You may have to reach up ☐ to replace a burned-out ☐.

1. high   2. light

What's the story about?

Flora Perez lived in the country. One Wednesday morning in February, she was surprised to see fresh white snow shining in the bright sunlight. She turned on the radio and listened.

The announcer said that there would be no school that day.

"This will give us a chance to take a ride in a sleigh," said Flora's mother, walking into the room.

"Hurrah!" shouted Flora.

The whole family climbed into the sleigh. They wrapped warm blankets round their feet. Flora's father held the reins tight. They waved to their neighbors as the sleigh moved straight and fast over the snow. It was a delightful ride for the Perez family.

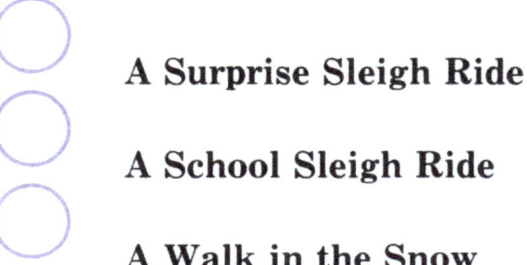

○ A Surprise Sleigh Ride

○ A School Sleigh Ride

○ A Walk in the Snow

Father bought me a book about the life of Abraham Lincoln. Reading the book taught me many things I had not known about this great man. He was the sixteenth president of the United States. He was president when the war was fought between the North and the South. He believed that neighbor should love neighbor, and he wanted all men to be free. He was often called "Honest Abe." When he was killed, men knew they had lost a great president.

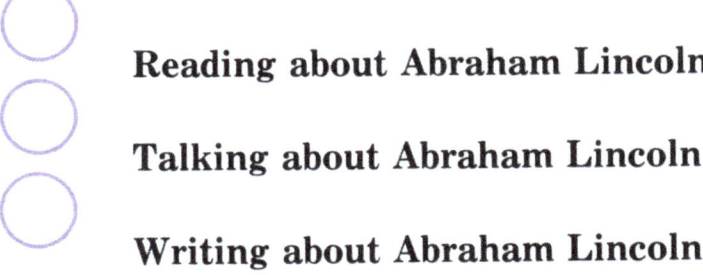

○ Reading about Abraham Lincoln

○ Talking about Abraham Lincoln

○ Writing about Abraham Lincoln

4

If it's nighttime, what could you use?

If it's nighttime and you want to sleep, what could you use?

- ○ a nightgown
- ○ half an orange
- ○ a bright light

If it's the night before a test, what could you use?

- ○ ribbon and scissors
- ○ a cheerful rhyme
- ○ a walk in the sunlight

If it's nighttime and you want to walk outside, what could you use?

- ○ a bright flashlight
- ○ a handkerchief
- ○ some furniture

If it's daytime, what could you use?

If it's daytime and you're lost on an island, what could you use?

- ○ a box of crumbs
- ○ the moonlight
- ○ a friendly guide

If it's daytime and you're in school, what could you use?

- ○ a piece of chalk
- ○ a clothesline
- ○ a wrong answer

If you're outside on a snowy day, what could you use?

- ○ a large sleigh
- ○ some summer clothes
- ○ a frightening picture

The Sailors Head for an Island

Bill and his friends often pretended they were sailors on a ship taking them to a distant island. They brought large bottles of water for their journey, but no food. They thought it would be fun to fish for their own food.

"The waters are full of salmon," said Bill. "If we catch enough of them, we certainly will not be hungry on our trip."

After two days at sea, Bill sighted a ship. They found that the other ship was friendly.

When night came, the stars guided Bill toward the unknown island. The moon shone brightly and lighted the way in the night. Bill wrote about the whole day's journey on writing paper he had brought with him.

The next morning they sighted the island in the distance. It seemed to have high hills. The boys were about to climb over the ship's rail and onto the island beach, when a noise startled them.

"What was that?" Bill asked.

"It's your mother, Bill," his friend answered.

"Come and get your supper, Bill," his mother called.

It was the end of the voyage for that day, but they were certain that they would take another trip soon.

	Yes	No
1. The boys were pretending to be sailors in a scene for a play at school.	○	○
2. The sailors were on a voyage to a faraway island.	○	○
3. The sailors thought the ship approaching them was an enemy ship.	○	○
4. When Bill and his friends pretended to be sailors, they often brought food.	○	○
5. At night Bill wrote about the day's trip on writing paper he had brought with him.	○	○
6. The sailors reached the island at suppertime and ate in a castle high on a hill.	○	○

4

I wear khaki clothes.

I am taught to stand up straight and to march.

Sometimes I have to stand at attention.

Am I — a sidewalk / a soldier / a sleigh

It is sharp, and is used to slice fruit.

It is dangerous if you aren't taught to use it properly.

Because it's sharp, young children aren't allowed to use it.

Is it — a knife / a knee / a knock

Women and girls put it on at night when they're getting ready for bed.

Its colors can be bright or light.

It can be made of cotton.

Is it — a light bulb / a nightgown / a clothesline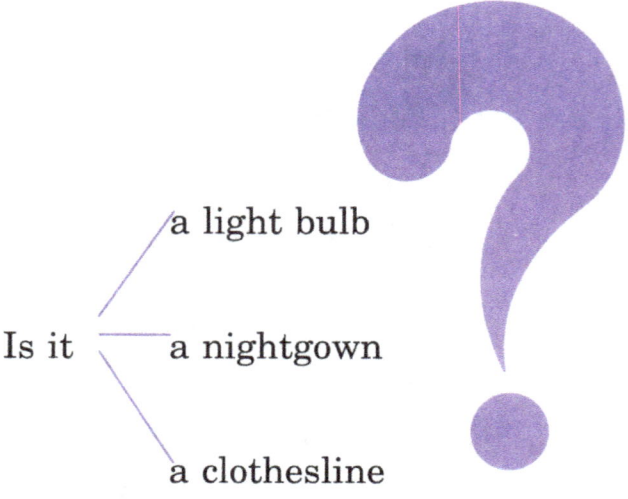

www.ingramcontent.com/pod-product-compliance
Lightning Source LLC
LaVergne TN
LVHW060212080526
838202LV00052B/4260